DARK PSYCHOLOGY
SECRETS

Techniques of manipulation and mind control, get the
art of reading people through human behavior 101,
learn the Practical Uses and Defenses of persuasion,
and brainwashing

Tony Clark

Table of Contents

INTRODUCTION

Why the psychological impression of any threat causes living being the reaction? The appropriate response is in human life systems, all the more precisely, in the reasons of torment showing up. Is psychological agony like a physical one?

How does agony happen? With physical suffering, everything is visible. We don't think about simple motor reflexes that are performed leveled out of spinal rope.

During physical receptor sensation, the anxious motivation is transmitted using nerves to comparing cerebrum part. At that point, the mind transmits a reaction drive to an organ. Happens to feel of agony, as it were klendusity is reacting.

How psychological torment happens? Our living being has such element as self-guideline of every single physiological procedure, as such, mind reactions on the adjustment in the substance forms in the life form.

Likely, affected by feelings in the creature happens some progress, for instance, in blood organization, at that point it is transmitted to the cerebrum, and again the reaction motivation from the mind is transferred to one of the organs, and consequently, torment happens. Give it a chance to call the psychological reason for the agony.

Presently we ought to see how feelings effect on the physical state of a living being. It is essential to comprehend the confused association both of sensory system and attitude. For that reason, there is a need in authority.

For instance, when you dread obscurity, you experience the ill effects of anguish, woodiness in bloom, distress in the throat. You feel like someone stops your breath. Here you dread not murkiness itself but rather a thing that can remain in the dimness. It depends on got data about it during your life. You dread that something can play the fiend with you. A little kid never fears haziness until he was determined what can be in it. Give it a chance to call cognizant dread.

Such fears as the dread of a substantial circumstance or article that startles you with something and rises the sentiment of dread and loathsomeness additionally allude to cognizant terror since you feel this dread in the aftereffect of your terrible experience or harmful data got from somebody. What is the idea of this dread? How does this dread happen? What do I feel? Absence of certainty. Shame. Disheartening. Dormancy. Uneasiness. Fault. Damage. Shock. Stress. Frenzy. You feel trouble in your bloom. Respiratory difficulty. Cold sweat. These are psychological and physical sensations in your body. Furthermore, that implies that dread is interconnected with other negative feelings. One thing causes another, originates from the other, however, suggests one and something very similar.

Shouldn't something be said about oblivious dread or a pure dread not founded on the experience? What would it be able to be?

This can be the dread of the vulnerability, fear of the unidentified. For instance, kids dread clamors, unknown things. For the most part, from the earliest starting point of human history, individuals consistently were scared of baffling demonstrations of nature. Or on the other hand, their dread depended on marvel seen previously?

For instance, the dread of unknown future, fear of conceivable fantasized adverse occasions. How would we discover that these are awful occasions? We contrast potential occurrences and experienced negative ones.

For reasons unknown, we dread strange things since we dread terrible strange things. We don't fear well-hidden things since they excite happiness. Furthermore, when we feel dread, every single right occasion we do overlook. At the end of the day, when we consider an unknown time in our mind, an awful image shows up, thus happens a sentiment of dread dependent on harmful early experienced terror. It implies that the fear of an unknown thing is a conscious dread.

Chapter one
Dark Psychology Defined

Dark Psychology is the investigation of the human condition as it identifies with the mental idea of individuals to go after other individuals propelled by criminal and additionally freak drives that need a reason and general suppositions of instinctual drives and sociology hypothesis. All of humankind can deceive different people and living animals. While many limits or sublimate this propensity, some follow up on these driving forces.

Dark Psychology looks to comprehend those musings, sentiments, observations, and abstract handling frameworks that lead to savage conduct that is contradictory to contemporary understandings of human behavior. Dark Psychology expects that criminal, freak, and harsh practices are purposive and have some objective, objective situated inspiration 99.99% of the time. It is the staying .01%, Dark Psychology parts from Adlerian hypothesis and the Teleology. Dark Psychology proposes there is a district inside the human mind that empowers a few people to submit terrible acts without reason. In this hypothesis, it has been begotten the Dark Singularity.

Dark Psychology places that all humanity has a repository of vindictive aim towards others going from negligibly prominent and short-lived musings to unadulterated psychopathic degenerate practices with no strong objectivity. This is known as the Dark Continuum. Moderating components going about as accelerants as well as attractants to moving toward the Dark Singularity, and where an individual's horrifying activities fall on the Dark Continuum, is the thing that Dark Psychology calls Dark Factor. Brief acquaintances with these ideas are delineated beneath. Dark Psychology is an idea this author has thought about for a long time. It has just been as of late that he has at last conceptualized the definition, reasoning, and psychology of this part of the human condition. Dark Psychology sets some individuals to submit these similar demonstrations and do as such not for influence, cash, sex, requital, or some other known reason. They offer these ghastly demonstrations without an objective. Improved, their closures don't legitimize their methods. Some individuals damage and harm others for doing as such. Inside in every last one of us is this potential. A possibility to hurt others without cause, clarification, or intention is the territory this essayist investigates. Dark Psychology expects this dark potential is fantastically intricate and significantly progressively hard to characterize.

Dark Psychology accepts we as a whole have the potential for predatory practices, and this potential approaches our considerations, emotions, and recognitions. As you will peruse all through this original copy, we as a whole have this potential, yet just a couple of us follows upon them. We all have had considerations and emotions, at some time, of needing to carry on cruelly. We, as a whole, have had musings of needing to hurt others seriously without kindness. When you are straightforward with yourself, you should concur you have had considerations and feeling of needing to submit offensive acts.

Given the reality, we see ourselves as generous animal categories; one might want to accept we figure these contemplations and emotions would be non-existent. Sadly, we as a whole have these considerations, and fortunately, never follow up on them. Dark Psychology presents some individuals have these equivalent considerations, sentiments, and observations, yet follow up on them in either planned or indiscreet ways. The undeniable distinction is they follow up on them while others have brief considerations and sentiments of doing as such.

Dark Psychology places that this predator style is purposive and has some balanced, objective situated inspiration. Religion, theory, psychology, and different authoritative opinions have endeavored fittingly to characterize Dark Psychology. It is genuine most human conduct, identified with abhorrence activities, is purposive and objective situated. However, Dark Psychology accepts there is a territory where purposive manner and objective arranged inspiration appears to wind up indistinct. There is a continuum of Dark Psychology exploitation going from contemplations to an unadulterated psychopathic abnormality with no evident discernment or reason. This continuum, Dark Continuum, conceptualizes the way of thinking of Dark Psychology.

Dark Psychology tends to that piece of the human mind or all-general human condition that takes into account and may even affect ruthless conduct. A few attributes of this conduct propensity are, as a rule, its absence of bright regular inspiration, its all-inclusiveness, and its lack of consistency. Dark Psychology expects this all-inclusive human condition is extraordinary or augmentation of advancement. Give us a chance to take a gander at some exceptionally essential principles of improvement. In the first place, consider we advanced from different creatures, and we directly are the perfection of all creature life. Our frontal flap has enabled us to turn into the pinnacle animal. Presently given us a chance to accept that being summit animals does not make us expelled from our creature senses and savage nature.

10 Psychology Tricks to Get People to Do What You Want

1. Response to generosity, or Benjamin Franklin effect

History tells us that Benjamin Franklin needed to become friends with an individual who did not, by any means like him. This individual was searching for a rare book, which Franklin had. At the point when Benjamin found out about this, he let this individual acquire this unusual book, and when the book came back to the proprietor, Benjamin just expressed gratitude toward him. Thus, they turned out to be the closest companions.

2. Take a stab at requesting more than you need to get.

This thought is straightforward and is likened to exchanging available. This will never neglect to work for you. You need to expand your needs if you are necessary to somebody. In the first place, you will no doubt get can't. Try not to surrender and give it some time. In 95% of cases, the individual who is keen on you will in the long run react and offer somewhat less than you initially requested, yet it is destined to be higher than you at first needed to get.

3. Molded want to help

This thought is fundamentally the same as the past one. To cause somebody to have a bona fide and unyielding want to assist you, with asking them once to accomplish something for you that they may not have the capacity to do. Having been cannot, you have made for yourself an individual who will feel inferable from you. Doubtlessly, they will have a craving for helping you on different occasions since they will have a blameworthy sentiment of not having the option to help in any case.

4. Continuously compliment

Complimenting is universal. First off, figure out how to comprehend that sweet talk should look common, else it might bring more negative results than positive.

When you attempt to play along to somebody who has high confidence, at that point, you have better shots in succeeding. Individuals of this sort love themselves and love honeyed words, and they don't appear to see it. The individuals who have low confidence may see craftiness and double-dealing when you attempt to make them feel much improved.

5. Mirror

When you need to be preferred by somebody, attempt to imitate them, people having these attributes are treated continuously by society as chameleons, when it is recognizable how they always show signs of change and acclimate to each new individual they meet. This ability can be a helpful instrument to pull in suitable individuals who are essential to you.

This guideline is regular among comics and bosses of spoof. The majority of the famous people who have been satirizing on TV screens are frequently good companions to these on-screen characters and comics.

6. Request benevolence from the individuals who are drained

When somebody is drained, the individual in question is progressively receptive to your solicitations. The appropriate response lies in the way that when individuals get worn out, they are depleted physically, however regularly rationally. If your supervisor is worn out, the person can without much of a stretch enable you to complete your work the following day, which you should complete on schedule and with quality. This will include more regard and acclaim from your supervisor, primarily because you stayed faithful to your commitment and respectability.

7. Start by requesting little supports

, Request a little supports before all else, and you will probably open the door for more credit. As indicated by this standard, individuals frequently turned out to be needy while taking an interest in volunteerism. For instance, from the outset, you might be approached to participate in the development against deforestation, which you support, at that point, react to an ever-increasing number of solicitations. It is a little support. However, you are step by step molded to give more. All of a sudden, you are prepared to help endeavors against deforestation in inaccessible Tanzania or join some "green" gathering and make commitments.

8. Do whatever it takes not to address individuals if they are incorrect

In his reality known book, Dale Carnegie recommends not to criticize individuals for their obvious human blunders, in any event not when you have recently found those. If you are worried about other individuals' illegitimacy, approach it in all respects, cautiously. Regardless of whether you are looked with a grumbler, who accuses his inconveniences of everyone except himself, don't yell it in his face. Attempt to concur with his assessment for the present, and after that bit by bit, attempt to change this perspective. Else, you may confront the danger of turning into his most exceedingly awful adversary.

9. Rehash expressions and articulations of individuals who are imperative to you

This standard takes after the rule of "chameleon" when individuals copy signals and outward appearances of the individual, whom they are keen on or whom they esteem. Words can be charming to the ear, if they sound like a vibration. Have a go at saying what this individual has just referenced, what he had expertly played in his mind.

10. Gesturing makes a difference

Researchers found that when individuals gesture while tuning in to somebody, they no doubt will, in general, concur with the speaker. They additionally discovered that when somebody gestures before somebody talking, the individual who speaks, much like a parrot, will rehash similar words again and again. In this manner, gesturing incites audience's genuine understanding.

How People Are Manipulated Emotionally and Why

Passionate or mental control intends to impact the conduct of someone else by specific strategies which may not be apparent to the controlled or even to other people. The target may not be to change the behavior of the controlled individual yet, also, to make him persuaded that there is no other method to escape the circumstance or that his association with the controller is unavoidable. It is a type of maltreatment. However, it may not be as apparent as different structures. Passionate control is psychological mistreatment which might be related to different kinds of abuse, for example, physical and sexual maltreatment.

There is a distinction between influence and passionate control. Power isn't coercive and regards the privilege of the individual to pick and to acknowledge or decline the proposed conduct. In power, it might appear to be externally that the individual is permitted to choose. Notwithstanding, under the shallow misrepresentation of the opportunity of decision, there is an undercurrent of passionate compulsion.

The procedure of passionate control includes two gatherings: the controller and the controlled in the process of power, which has its very own elements.

The Manipulator:

Controllers lie on a range of various characters. They are altogether described by variation from the norm in nature. It is anything but difficult to recognize the heartless, unfeeling, insensitive, and callous insane person. Nonetheless, some other cluttered characters may utilize control to endure their pathology and keep up their mental uprightness. A sincerely dependent individual may look for his enthusiastic needs by controlling others. The equivalent with the narcissistic character when somebody has a go at satisfying their desire for power, prestige, vanity, and self-magnification by controlling others. The theatrical which is looking for attention, extravagance, fulfillment of shallow enthusiastic and sexual needs may utilize all their tempting and emotional embellishments to control others. Individuals with Borderline character with their confusing feelings and feeling of inward void, emotional episodes, rash undertakings, and carrying on will control others even by their hatred or self-hurt.

The controller attempts to control the controlled to keep up his enthusiastic or individual increases. A few controllers can without much of a stretch move their concentration starting with one unfortunate casualty then onto the next yet others my battle as far as possible to hold their injured individual under their hooks.

The Manipulated:

Few out of every odd one can be effectively controlled. This is consistent with some degree, even though an astute insane person can threaten the least powerless by strategies of dread.

The most helpless against control are those serene and hesitant people who lack fearlessness. They are generally honest, accommodating, fair, or once in a while, guileless. They might be forgotten people, damaged and looking for shelter in the hands of the reliable controller. They may lack confidence, with a profound feeling of blame, which is scanning for discipline and an inclination that they should have the right to be rebuffed.

Indeed, even the individuals who can intellectualize their life problems may mislead themselves by working their mind hard into the shrouded justifiable explanations behind the controller to act along these lines. They discover excuses for the culprit, yet they disregard excuses to liberate themselves from the hands of the controller. They appreciate intellectualizing their enduring as they find out confronting their powerlessness too excruciating to even think about living with.

The Manipulation Process:

Various strategies are utilized in the control procedure. Some are plain, and others are too unpretentious to even think about exploring or too complex to also consider analyzing.

1. Instillation of Guilt:

Blame is a substantial negative spark. Controllers know by experience that their exploited people can feel regretful effectively. They see that the injured individual even admit his shortcomings and apologizes and feels humiliated pointlessly. Steadily, they make the unfortunate casualty accepts they are bad enough, they couldn't care less enough, or they are egotistical, brutal, exploitative, and even parasitic. Indeed, as a rule, the controller has a large portion of these highlights. The unfortunate casualty can not look judiciously to see this isn't accurate because he/she has been modified into self-question, self-fault, and admiration of others together with devaluation of self.

2. Disgracing:

A controller uses strategies to make the injured individual feels despicable, dishonorable, and insufficient so that there will never be a way out. When the unfortunate casualty attempts to challenge a controller, the last makes the injured individual feels embarrassed by terrorizing, dread, blame and self-question, with an allegation of lack of capacity to do anything, lack of stamina, of power or mental fortitude. Mockery, jokes, criticism, and negative remarks, or even just dangers might be utilized. Once in a while, the controller incites the unfortunate casualty into a demonstration of hostility out of dissatisfaction and agony. This usually neglects to free the person in question. In any case, the controller would utilize such occurrence to make the unfortunate casualty feels further disgrace, disappointment, and blame.

3. Picking up Sympathy:

The controller may play the job of the unfortunate casualty to pick up compassion and collaboration if different strategies fall flat. Summoning empathy, pity, and kindness from somebody honest aren't troublesome in that capacity people can not stand seeing somebody who is enduring or in agony. The controller continues bemoaning how unfortunate they are, the way unreasonable things are, and how they are casualties of such coldblooded life.

4. Terrorizing:

Dangers might be unmistakable or clandestine. A scary look, disregarding the other individual, articulation of displeasure or objection are a portion of the creepy demonstrations. At times, it is faking rage and a blast of feeling which is utilized to threaten the individual into accommodation. Dangers may go from outrageous conduct to destroy the economic wellbeing of the unfortunate casualty up to physical assaults and now and again dangers to execute.

5. Enchantment:

Sexual control is utilized to give a misguided feeling of closeness and guarantee the obligation of the relationship. Passionate temptation by honeyed words, acclaim, and enchanting disposition can be quickly used to make the unfortunate casualties bring down their safeguards and addition their trust. This usually is brief and flighty, and through such irregular uplifting feedback, the injured individual is guided into the round of control.

6. Lying:

Lying is at the center of control either by retention a lot of reality, excluding some significant certainties, or manufacturing false stories. The controller may overstate or limit actualities, cheat and hoodwink the person in question and construct an incredible picture of himself, his unfortunate casualty and their relationship. Faking is another type of viable lying. The controller may deny that he has done anything incorrectly purposefully or that he was unconscious of the impact on the person in question or may put on a look of amazement or resentment. Distinct lying through denying "what you are discussing?" or claiming to be distracted or confounded is once in a while utilized. Faking sickness or pain, fainting or false fits might be used to pick up compassion and debilitate the safeguards of the person in question.

7. Justification:

The controller may utilize various moves to clarify the explanations behind his conduct, which use the powerlessness of the person in question. If the unfortunate casualty is guileless or unfit to pass judgment on a contention fundamentally, the controller may utilize a large number of the misrepresentations of rationale to beat his injured individual's counter-contentions. When the unfortunate casualty is ridden with blame, disgrace or brutal soul, the controller uses all contentions which advance to such vulnerabilities.

8. Refusal:

The controller may obtusely deny any wrongdoing or decline to let it out or dodge talking about the subject inside and out. He/she may participate in a drifting, superfluous befuddling talk which may redirect the attention to a shocking matter. Refusal is unique about lying if the individual is unconscious somewhat or entirely of reality.

9. Anticipating the fault:

The controller may extend the responsibility on the person in question, blaming him for his very own considerable lot indecencies or at times denounce other people who have wronged him for a mind-blowing duration and who made him what he is. The injured individual may feel either blame, or he is put on edge to account for himself, or he may feel compassion and distress for the controller.

10. Hostility:

The controller may depend on real hatred and brutality to cause the injured individual to submit to his will, specifically if the unfortunate casualty is flimsier or crippled. This may leave an unexpected in a faked upheaval of indignation or extreme anger. Any reaction of a comparative sort from the injured individual is looked with increasingly intense animosity which might be later accused on the unfortunate casualty himself, or a created disease might be charged with just ascribed to the enthusiastic issues the controller professes to confront.

How to Manipulate - Mind Manipulation

Instructions to control and doing mind control is an ability that is inborn to every one of us. Everyone is brought into the world with it. Every individual responds and cooperates. That is how the control works in the general public. It acquires individuals and out. It is how we speak with each other.

The most effective method to control is as significant as how to convey and identify with individuals. When we relate and pass on our contemplations to our friends, we draw them to hear us out and comprehend our very own convictions if not consent to it. We base our prosperity on how individuals react to the sort of reasoning that we have. When we get good reactions from individuals, we will feel fulfilled, and that fulfillment develops our entire being. If we some way or another neglect to be comprehended, we regularly resort to contentions because of our intuitive battles for the manipulative strategies of others. We would prefer not to be controlled yet some way or another we will, in general overlook that each choice and moves that we make are just results of mind control by others.

The saddest part is that we regularly neglect to understand that we have to control to endure and to be effective. When we go for survival, we don't have to rehearse a ton of mind control systems. Would it be a good idea for us to settle down for less? We need to turn out to be more than and more significant than ourselves.

The first thing we have to consider is that we have to comprehend that control isn't harmful. By one way or another, negative meanings sway how we manage individuals. We thought, being dull and direct about telling others our need is a sort of control and in this manner is terrible. We believed that when we request that somebody do the things our way is a sort of power, then we shun attempting to seek help. We then neglect to understand that we pass up on the opportunity that could have been another entryway for a chance.

We invest a lot heavily for ourselves about doing playing reasonably while the world isn't. What we are doing whatever it takes not to trap everybody and mean them awful. We prefer to open our eyes on the open doors that are merely anticipating to be opened. When we set up a mixed drink party since we need to welcome and be familiar with someone who we know can enable us to well with our advantage is a sort of system that we need.

Mind control is inside us. We needn't bother with the extraordinary psychic capacity to have the option to control individuals and be fruitful. We need to know the procedures and skillfully practice it.

Manipulation in Relationships

Photoshop or computerized picture altering programming is utilized to control pictures to appear to be unique from the first or to give the image a look which you want. Control is the same, and it's tied in with controlling an individual or a circumstance to get what you need. Why? A lot of things could cause this conduct.

Do you end up doing things that you would prefer indeed not to? When somebody near you or in power recommends that you accomplish something without wanting to, how would you feel?

Individuals use control as a method for controlling individuals, occasions, and their very own lives. It's a sort of self-preservation component. As a rule, these individuals who attempt manipulative traps had no control as little children, frequently manhandled or relinquished, and so on. Or on the other hand, in adulthood, they accept authority is a method for getting what they need. Utilizing the trap gives them power, and power feels euphoric.

Checkmate is a game position in chess where a players best is undermined with catch, and there is no real way to counter the risk. Or then again, basically, the lord is under direct assault and can't abstain from being caught. Comparable is the round of control, to make a circumstance wherein the other individual is found and deceived.

To control somebody is to play with somebody's psyche. You attempt to persuade the other individual that what you are proposing is the best choice for him. However, you realize it will work to support you.

For instance when Zora revealed to her mother she would go to her in-laws place in the event that she is a weight for them, she realized what will be the answer from her folks and she got what she needed and just remained for a considerable length of time together by making her parents feel remorseful of requesting that her return to her home.

The manipulator sees himself at the focal point of the universe, and different things rotate around him. He is content with the feeling of proprietorship and ownership of everything, feels little sympathy for other people, and does little for others except if there is close to a home favorable position.

Try to remember it and guarantee that you are neither a manipulator nor being controlled, as this speaks to a broken relationship. Here are a couple of approaches to know whether somebody is attempting to control you:

1. Tears: When somebody wells up with tears in his eyes, it doesn't mean their authentic tears.

2. Discipline: Withdrawing affection and backing.

3. Falsehood: Manipulators are talented liars. They make up sensible stories to make individuals feel frustrated about them so they can get something.

4. Redirection: Manipulator not giving a straight response to a straight inquiry and directing the discussion to another theme.

5. Flattering You: To get their direction, manipulators will frequently make you feel better with the goal that they would then be able to request that you accomplish something that they need.

6. Outrage: Manipulator uses scandal for enthusiastic power to get the injured individual into accommodation.

7. Remorseful fit: This manipulative conduct looks to make you feel regretful.

To recognize manipulative practices, consider what they do and whether their words are utilized to get you to accomplish something that you honestly would prefer not to do. Pose yourself a couple of inquiries about the reason for their activities.

When you recognize the manipulator, settle on an insightful decision of either cutting off from him or overlook him. Remain your ground and don't endeavor to turn and figure out how to state 'No.'

Manipulation in Relationships - The Seven Psychological Buttons on Our Backs

Is it accurate to say that you are particularly helpless against control? Or then again, are you worried by feeling continual like you are moving to somebody's strings. Perhaps at work, at home, or among your 'companions'. Always manipulated people will, in general, have a scope of related character styles that are both recognized and utilized by controllers. These resemble catches of control for the controller. The initial step to lessening power in your life is to perceive the scores in you.

What are the primary mental catches?

1 Having a substantial requirement for endorsement and acknowledgment

About everybody needs to be enjoyed and acknowledged. That is sound and typical. Numerous people, maybe on account of their hereditary foundation as well as living conditions, have a lot higher requirement for endorsement than others. The higher your need, the more inclined you are to control.

A controller may keep those with a substantial requirement for endorsement in a steady condition of uneasiness by never paying you compliments or discovering anything significant in what you do. Consider yourself buckling down the entire day to get a spur of the moment gesture of congratulations, or to get a trashing comment around one minor deficiency after a whole stack of incredible work.

2 Fearing negative feelings

A few people are delicate to substantial pessimistic feelings, strife, or showdown. This implies they change their conduct to maintain a strategic distance from the annoyance or struggle. Almost consistently at an expense to themselves or somebody, they are speaking to.

A few controllers intentionally put on a furious look, or begin to raise their voice, basically to cause disarray or worry in their unfortunate casualty. Think about the whipped canine, that recoils when a hand is marginally raised. It makes itself little and low, changing its conduct, trying to diminish the apparent danger.

3 Being a people pleaser and hung up on being decent

There is nothing amiss with being pleasant. In any case, there is an issue when you continually overlook your very own requirements for other people. How would you know whether you are a people pleaser?

Do you burst into a free for all of the movement to help somebody since they referenced a need, at that point revile faintly about how brief period you need to complete your very own things? Do you give significantly more to others than is provided to you? At that point, you might be a people pleaser.

There is usually a substantial component of "if I am decent to others they won't hurt me" in endless people pleasers.

Shouldn't something is said about Mother Theresa? She gave a lot of herself for other people.

Mother Theresa was not a people pleaser (ask those she consulted with to get support for her endeavors). People like Mother Theresa help others all separate terms and are responsible for a lot of any connections.

4 Lacking confidence

If you think that it is hard to state no, you may experience the ill effects of an absence of emphatics. Inadequately decisive people are additionally prone to be people pleasers. You are in a difficult situation when you additionally have solid repugnance for negative sentiments also.

Frequently, an absence of emphatics is connected with affectability and dread of adverse reactions to your needs or needs. Saying no may make you feel on edge, apprehensive or awkward. Additionally, you may feel exasperated and angry with yourself for being exploited each time.

Numerous people have these sentiments somewhat, yet they state no in any case when it is suitable for them.

5 Having low self-dependence

People with low self-dependence are dubious about their judgment and capacities. Regularly, they have almost no self heading in their lives. In past generations, many married and exceptionally skilled ladies had decreased self-dependence as they had not been raised to hope to be their very own ace predetermination, particularly outside of the home.

People with low self-dependence can, for the most part, be spotted by how they always look for contribution to a large portion of their pending choices, regularly even basic ones.

Low self-dependence makes you a single imprint for a controller as they will be there to control and direct you.

You can anticipate that a controller should criticize your subject matters and any choices you make. Controllers will frequently rapidly direct you to zones of their fitness where they can exhibit their boundlessly predominant 'authority' and add to your sentiments of deficiency.

6 Feeling like you have little command over your predetermination

This is identified with low-self dependence; however, contrasts in that the individual feels the outside world has substantially more power over how their life turns out than they do. Conversely, people with a progressively inside center have a more noteworthy conviction that they have an enormous level of authority over what befalls them.

Having an external control perspective on the world makes you both defenseless against control and gloom.

A primary consideration in sorrow feels that you have practically no influence over a progressing terrible or hazardous circumstance. Being with a controller and accepting that you have little power over life is a formula for despair. Their controls and your convictions will lead you onto a way of learned helplessness.

7 Having an immature feeling of personality

Do you sense that you are relatively deficient and that your character is little and inconsequential contrasted and people around you? Are you dubious about who you indeed are and a big motivator for you? Do you carry on with your life increasingly through others (counting those on TV) than yourself?

Numerous people have had adolescence wherein their value was ceaselessly slandered. Or on the other hand, in their touchy youngsters, got ceaseless negative input and remarks. Such a foundation can stunt an individual's advancement and debilitate their feeling of personality.

To a controller, such people are a superb nebulous chunk of earth, after that they can make their very own structures. More often than not, to make you progressively consistent to their will and to get you to carry on with your life increasingly through them.

Free Poker Player Manipulation Example

You may pay $1000 Buy-in; you may play free poker; however, what you don't do is play your cards. You are likewise playing with, or rather you are endeavoring to impact different players at the table, so they do what you need. Your goal is that they give to your stack!

Playing the player has two sides. Concerning your play, you are attempting to peruse different players, read their playstyle, figure their feelings and drivers, and from here play your cards ideally.

On the rival player side, you are attempting to play them to expand the level of mistake with which they order your style of play, inspirations, and activities.

To figure out how to do this, let's take a gander at a case of playing the player in real life from a WSOP occasion.

- BLINDS 50k/100k

- A has Ac-Qh raises 350k

- Bis on huge visually impaired has Kc-Js, calls 230k (Pot 880k)

K-J is typically somewhat frail to call a raise. Also, B doesn't have position over A, yet he calls since he needs A to figure.

From the enormous visually impaired, by and large, we call since we are on a rebate, so we may have 6-5, 10-8, and a lot of other uncertain hands which require speculating.

- FLOP 4d-5h-3d

- B wagers 535k

Since little cards fell, B currently needs A to feel that his call from the huge visually impaired hit the Flop and that his hand may well incorporate those uncertain hands like 5-4, 8-5, or even 6-7, or two Diamonds. What did A think?

- A raises to 1.8m (Pot 3.215m)

- B needs 1.265m to call.

Here, An idea that B's wagered was only a continuation wagered, and with little cards falling A's conviction is fortified that B merely is attempting to complete the hand. How might small cards likely hit B?

Furthermore, B has been playing forcefully throughout the night (taking pots, and so forth.) so B could be wagering with something (which isn't likely with little cards falling) or with nothing. B could be playing pretty much anything, particularly from the enormous visually impaired.

By then, A bet that B has nothing. He could likewise have evaluated that when B had something and stakes everything later; at that point, he can move out quick. So he raised to attempt B's quality.

B folds

B folds, because, to be sure, he has nothing, and when he calls, he will be resolved to proceed. Had B moved in with no reservations then it will be a decent holding nothing back, for A could, in any case, be speculating this point what B's hand was. B's cards were not sufficient.

Likewise, the creases, because A raised from late position, which takes into account a more extensive scope of hands, as even 5-4 or two Diamonds.

Poker, undoubtedly, isn't just a round of good hands versus great hands. Experienced poker players will win with awful hands under the right conditions.

We offer credit to B for first attempting to win with a terrible hand, a great exertion to play the player.

Sadly for B, A did the playing the player task radiantly as well, having noted past activities and inspirations and related that to current con content and likelihood thus happened to win well.

End

It requires some investment to figure out how to play poker on the web or disconnected at a level over the careless, uneducated "chip tossing" seen at numerous tables when you play free poker.

Most players will never go this kind of exertion to figure out how to play poker, they simply want to utilize fundamental thoughts and trust in karma - and when you depend on karma, at that point karma without a doubt will lead your game and you will never add up to quite a bit of a poker player.

Along these lines, if you do have poker desire, put aside loads of time to figure out how to play poker well. Methodology, for example, we talk about in this section is a crucial piece of things. Ensure you consider what you are playing and why and how that may influence different player's impression of you and your hand - and afterward attempt and degrade it to further your potential benefit!

Psychological Manipulation - How to Protect Yourself From Psychological Manipulation

If you feel that mental control occurs in motion pictures and cross-examination rooms, reconsider. It's something that can without much of a stretch invade your regular day to day existence. You may encounter it from work, school, or even while you're out purchasing food supplies at the general store.

In all actuality, being controlled to purchase chicken rather than meat probably won't sound like such a major ordeal, however, shouldn't something be said about harassing in school or at work? These mental control strategies frequently deteriorate as time passes by.

Except if you make a move and secure yourself, these circumstances may, in the long run, lead to unsafe impacts on your psychological, passionate, and physical wellbeing!

Know

Francis Bacon said that learning is control. Also, he's unquestionably directly about this one. By equipping yourself with data or by merely monitoring mental power, you are as of now securing yourself!

By what another method would you be able to take care of an issue if you don't know there would one say one is in the first place? Indeed, merely being the place you are at present and perusing this part as of now sends you three or four stages in front of your concern!

Adhere to Your Guns

This truly isn't the least hard thing on the planet to do. Some of the time, you can't resist the urge to be influenced by other individuals. Nonetheless, realize that once you fight the temptation to tail someone else's lead, it will all be justified, despite all the trouble.

You will get the sentiment of defeating something enormous, and you'll even observe yourself in another light, which thus, will serve to engage you more. This isn't equivalent to being very stubborn, as you may have guessed.

Develop Yourself

Focuses on mental control are as a rule the individuals who don't generally have a great deal of trust in themselves.

When you have much uncertainty, other individuals will attempt to utilize your absence of fearlessness to control you.

For instance, in case you're someone who thinks a ton about your appearance, someone else can without much of a stretch say something to trigger a response from you.

To anticipate being misled by such strategies, ensure you're alright with your identity. Search for all your great focuses as opposed to harping on your not all that great attributes. Be thankful for all the incredible things occurring in your life.

Try not to give mental control a chance to get to you. Moving to another school or exiting your profession isn't the answer to your concern. Fleeing won't enable you to go anyplace. All you get is a difference in condition; however, not a difference in outlook. Make sure to be alert on your toes, be uncompromising with your choices, and have confidence in yourself!

Chapter two

The Ultimate Guide to Improving Your Persuasion Techniques

The intensity of influence can open entryways for you and make the way to progress much smoother. After perusing this section, you will have a variety of persuasive techniques available to you.

The most persuasive techniques have their foundations in NLP (neuro-etymological programming). These influence techniques depend on compassion - to convince somebody - you should get them.

Compassion-Based Persuasive Techniques

The first and most significant thing you should comprehend about the individual you are attempting to impact is the thing that their mind best reacts to - feel, visual or sound-related incitement. Realizing this will enable you to be increasingly persuasive by connecting to and bolstering this particular want.

Females, for the most part, react best to emotions, however not generally. Men regularly respond well to visuals, and a few people are influenced by sound. To realize which is the best incitement to center your influence, take a gander at how they talk. Do they say "I see," "I hear what no doubt about it," "I feel that..."? These are evident instances. The right answer could be increasingly unobtrusive and maybe a blend of two kinds of incitement.

Change your influence techniques dependent on the sort of mind you are managing; for instance, when inducing somebody who is "feel" orientated, center around how they will feel if they do what you are attempting to persuade them to. Try not to attempt to disclose to them what it will resemble - you need to make them feel it.

The more you're mindful of the individual you're managing, the more adequately you will most likely center your persuasive techniques.

Mirror-Based Persuasive Techniques

Coordinating your non-verbal communication and even your posture/position is a simple however shockingly fantastic persuasive method. You should be inconspicuous, and it might feel cumbersome from the outset, yet with some training, you will perceive how compelling this system, known as "mirroring," can be at building up an affinity and facilitating persuasion. As well as centering the substance of your influence in a manner that interfaces well with their particular character type, you can likewise modify your language and the method in which you address put yourself on their level. Individuals react better to persuasive techniques that are in their own "language." Get on exact words that they use and use them back on them, particularly descriptive words. Focus on their speed, pitch, and volume, and react as correspondingly as could be allowed.

Other Persuasive Techniques

There are numerous other persuasive techniques that you can take a shot at and develop. We prescribe that you ace the compassion/mirror persuasive techniques above all as these are the best. In any case, the accompanying techniques can be essential augmentations to your influence armory.

PERSUASIVE WORDS

There are many subliminal persuasive words that one can utilize. Regularly there will be a suggestion to take action: for instance, "Do that" or "Be this." Positive words and modifiers, for example, "Certainly," "Most," and "Powerful" are exceptionally persuasive all alone.

Use "now" words, for example, "today" or "right now" frequently to subliminally recommend criticalness.

Facetious QUESTIONS

Getting the individual to think for themselves is exceptionally spurring and can in this way be incredibly persuasive. Pose inquiries that draw in them, and they consequently turned out to be increasingly responsive. This will likewise enable you to get familiar with them. Frequently this will even persuade them that they are settling on the choice when in actuality you have directed them to this influence.

Eye to eye connection

It is profoundly essential to building up a decent affinity with the individual you are attempting to induce. Without eye to eye connection, this is incomprehensible. With a careful and non-undermining eye to eye connection, you can create trust. Include a real grin and influence will be a lot simpler.

BE PERSUASIVE BY CONNECTING EMOTIONALLY, NOT RATIONALLY

Anybody in legislative issues will let you know - individuals don't react normally. They react dependent on feelings. To induce somebody, you should interface with them inwardly.

Aristotle distinguished the three essential components of each persuasive contention:

Ethos: the validity, information, skill, stature, and expert of the individual attempting to convince.

Logos: the intrigue of rationale, reason, intellectual reasoning, information, and realities.

Tenderness: the intrigue to the feelings; the non-intellectual, non-thinking inspirations that influence choices and activities.

All layers are significant, yet it is maybe the passionate layer that holds the most intensity of influence. We are emotional creatures and are substantially more liable to be convinced by the guarantee of inclination high than the guarantee of "something being right."

Are Persuasion Techniques Moral?

You might believe that utilizing influence techniques is shameless, underhand. In reality, you may wind up with the difficulty of whether to use them on somebody you adore. It's truly up to you how you feel about utilizing persuasive techniques, yet recollect the accompanying.

Individuals ought to know about the techniques, and know when others are attempting to control them.

When you effectively influence somebody, you have out-contended them.

Influence is constantly discretionary. However, after much practice, you may find that these persuasive techniques implant into the idea of your being. Okay, feel remorseful for utilizing some other parts of your character, for example, talking unquestionably?

A significant part of the time, you will attempt to do what is best for them at any rate. The motivation behind interfacing with somebody sincerely is to realize what they need. When you know this, you are just convincing them to accomplish something that they will need to do at any rate. Along these lines, according to its, influence isn't controlled - it is merely bringing your point over.

Individuals ought to know enough to settle on their own choices. In a perfect world, you ought to be sure that you can utilize these persuasive techniques to make the wisest decision for all concerned.

Definition Of Persuasion

Persuasive abilities can surely be gained from disappointment. The most significant piece of understanding regret is by characterizing it. Distress is characterized by Giving up on the compelling procedure or merely taking a blind leap of faith without a blueprint. Suffering can likewise be described by not making it even though you did everything you should do; however, do everything a short time later to decide why the influence was not made. Whichever way you characterize disappointment persuasive techniques require structure and scripting to your procedure.

The dread of disappointment has ceased a more significant number of individuals before they have even begun than most different reasons. It's a similar reason that individuals continue working in a vocation that they loathe quite a long time after year. Ordinarily, business people will say the best thing that transpired is that they were terminated or lost employment that made them perform for another capacity. You will fight disappointment in either definition as long as you deal with your persuasive abilities.

So what does this have to do with influence achievement? Disappointment in some viewpoint or another isn't just ordinary; it is not out of the ordinary after some time. Indeed, even the best individuals in many businesses close at only 70%, that implies that they bomb 30% of the time or did they. Do you imagine that it irritates an individual to leave a discourse? This inquiry most likely is their concentrate long after their stimulating conversation even though they have let the torment of losing. They generally need to realize how to build their influence aptitudes.

The error is to give someone else a chance to characterize what a persuasive disappointment is to you into such an extent as should be obvious you that you are a disappointment. A lot of successful individuals still commit senseless errors every day they have quite recently lost spotlight on what they know works, or they have gotten sluggish.

Disappointment can be of advantage to you as an individual by discovering what doesn't work and what does.

What may work for a colleague or someone else does not imply that it will work for you, and that is OK too. Deals achievement originates from you discovering what works for you. Strong aptitudes for every individual might be diverse, relying on their abilities or potentially attitude. This is great news since you might probably discover persuasive skills to rule in your commercial center that others can't. This additionally clarifies why you have seen or heard other individuals do things that you can't copy even though you have attempted.

Achievement is a riddle for some since they enable it to be. For you to increase persuasive abilities, sometimes you should fall flat and approve of that. When you are terrified of accomplishment, you won't end up having it.

There is sooner or later where you must be powerless and even observed as helpless against developing in pretty much every part of your life — sometimes being powerless methods requesting help, falling flat or also not prevailing at the level that you need as well as want as soon or as quick as wanted.

There are a few people who will get to a point where they believe that they have fizzled. This is senseless additionally because as an individual, there will consistently be an undertaking that does not experience. Influence is a regularly changing and by not realizing that regardless of what number of successful techniques or persuasive aptitudes, you will fall flat. Your industry when it has not changed at this point it will soon that is exactly how business is advancement is a piece of every activity or enterprise.

Stopping Smoking - The Psychology Of Persuasion, Stopping Cigarettes

There is another field in advertising called influence brain science, the ability to get you to purchase what they need you to buy. This equivalent brain science is the thing that got you to begin smoking and can be utilized to enable you to stop cigarettes forever.

If you recall when you began smoking, there were explicit impacts. Family and companions commonly. You needed to fit in to be a piece of a gathering and be acknowledged.

Maybe you purchased the story that smoking made you look more established, or fresh or progressively modern. This was the point of considerable smoking organizations. Each had their very own picture.

The rough rancher on a pony, the tasteful lady or man wonderfully dressed frequently in a sumptuous environment. Our slamming through the wilderness in a four-wheel-drive just halting to illuminate a smoke.

Cigarette organizations lined up with games promoting, selling you a simple message that smoking and sports were perfect.

Hollywood demonstrated to us that it is so cool to smoke, how it appeared that possessing a scent like an ashtray was some way or another attractive and alluring.

Others purchased the message that smoking was an insubordinate activity. Their folks cautioned them about the risks, but then they rebel by smoking, putting insane the medical issues and many accept that it is possible that they will stop effectively when they are prepared or that they won't get malignancy.

A great many individuals were induced to smoke by some brain science, either purposefully on account of cigarette organizations or as a natural by-product through loved ones.

Fortunately, influence strategies can be utilized for both great and evil. You can rapidly be unpretentiously influenced to stop cigarettes. The best of these strategies is spellbinding.

Best of all, this procedure happens rapidly because, in the sleep-inducing state, learning is accomplished at a quickened rate. This happens because we bi-pass all the obstruction and uncertainty of the conscious personality.

We don't need to battle against the cognizant personalities recollections of the considerable number of accounts of individuals who discovered stopping smoking troublesome. In entrancing these accounts are of no intrigue, the oblivious personality unwinds and takes on the new data, and how about we go of the old.

It's somewhat similar to working with a PC, trash in trash out however great information in, at that point vast knowledge out, it's nearly as necessary as that, all that is required what's more is that you need the outcome.

Must-Learn Persuasion Techniques

The expression "persuasion" can mean plenty of things. On a comprehensive point of view, you can think of it as a piece of regular daily existence since the vast majority of us unknowingly apply persuasion in getting what we need or persuading someone else to accomplish something for us. Take, for instance, crafted by a sales rep; they regularly attempt to convince clients into purchasing their items, so they are utilizing distinctive "persuasion techniques" to persuade a client to do what they need - purchase the item. Indeed, even youthful individuals use persuasion techniques in persuading their folks to buy something for them. Then again, persuasion has more profound importance likewise. It can also allude to the ability to impart or impact the brain of someone else without getting took note. Individuals, in some cases, partner it with "enchantment," "mesmerizing," or "trap," or "power."

There are numerous kinds of persuasion techniques, and the most widely recognized ones are the accompanying: "name strategy," "positive language" method, "dull words" procedure, and" connecting" system.

Name system is a sort of persuasion strategy where a few individuals call an individual by their first name to stand out enough to be noticed and inevitably assemble compatibility. This can saw among sales reps who are attempting to persuade their clients to purchase their items. When they got the client's name, they more than once, state the client's name in a benevolent, totally persuading way.

Positive language is another ground-breaking persuasion procedure generally used. It alludes to the strategy of utilizing constructive, empowering, and exceedingly persuading words to induce someone else to concur with you or accomplish something for you.

Monotonous words procedure is where you use a word over and over until it is imparted in someone else's psyche and cause them to see things a similar way you do. It additionally uses the same language or highlight that the individual you are attempting to persuade is utilizing.

The connecting method is likewise a typical yet engaging system done by a large portion of us. We more often than not "make associations" with individuals and illuminate the individual we are attempting to persuade that we have usual companions and that we additionally know "Mr" or "Ms" "Famous", somebody that is significant and can enable us to accomplish our objective of affecting the individual to purchase our item, concur with us or get our administrations.

There's nothing incorrectly in utilizing persuasion techniques as long as your expectations are high. Persuasion techniques can be a great deal of assistance for some individuals and can complete an extreme change in an individual's life. Its essential objective is to persuade a person to disguise a thought or thought and consent to it!

Persuasion Techniques - 3 Powerful Laws of Persuasion

What amount are your words worth? Do individuals pay attention to you, or do they think about your recommendation while considering other factors? In this day and age, individuals are such a significant amount of harder to persuade. What's more, once in a while, your very activity relies upon how well you use persuasion techniques.

Regardless of whether it's requesting a raise or proposing another thought, you need persuasion techniques to help make you go. One approach to do that is by utilizing the laws of persuasion to further your potential benefit. Look at a portion of these techniques below.

Persuasion Technique # 1: The Law Of Friends

For reasons unknown, individuals are timid about asking for help from companions. They state that they would prefer not to exploit the kinship; yet at that point, what sort of companion would leave another companion in a difficult situation? This is the place one of the most dominant persuasion techniques depends on.

When you're companions with somebody, he/she will be bound to be influenced by you. For instance, When you state that espresso at a specific bistro is multiple times superior to anything your neighborhood espresso place, your companion will be effectively influenced into giving your suggested espresso a shot. You're not exploiting anyone here. That is only the everyday play of fellowship.

Persuasion Technique # 2: The Law Of Reciprocity

This specific persuasion system passes by numerous names. In one of Paulo Coelho's books, he considers it the support bank. So what is the support bank precisely? Simple. When you accomplish something beautiful for an individual, that individual is slanted to give back where its due. It's mostly an I-help-you-you-help-me circumstance.

This persuasion strategy is one of my top choices because it's necessary and direct. You don't need to play mind diversions or include other individuals into the set up to make it work.

Persuasion Technique # 3: The Law Of Consistency

Consistency is significant in the working environment. You can be decided about pretty brutally for saying one thing today and saying another tomorrow. This is one of the touchy persuasion techniques that expect you to be attentive and a decent audience.

Observe what your partners are stating about a specific task or a particular thought. Individuals who announce their situation on an issue will be bound to safeguard their side until the end. When you are sharp enough, you can use such a responsibility to further your potential benefit.

These persuasion techniques have been attempted and tried many, many occasions over. They depend on normal human responses and will commonly be successful anyplace.

Examples of Persuasion - 10 Tips For Treating a Pathological Liar

Everybody tells a little lie sooner or later in our lives, and that is merely human instinct. Indeed, even the instances of influence we'll discuss concur with that. Nonetheless, there are some that lie without need and can't resist the urge to recount stories that may not be valid. These individuals are known as neurotic liars, and the condition is as yet being contended over by specialists. Regardless of whether you accept that the state is genuine, the liars are apparent. These ten instances of influence and enticing tips will enable you to treat the propensity.

Tip 1: Long Term Psychotherapy

Chatting with a psychotherapist will assist the liar by finding the underlying driver of their condition. Simultaneously, it could likewise blowback and the liar feed the advisor with false stories.

Tip 2: Cognitive Behavior Therapy

Besides instances of influence, much like the typical treatment, this benevolent gives the patient bring home exercises, for example, journaling or artistry — these things the specialist can dissect and make sense of what is happening inside the individual.

Tip 3: Family and companion support

When the individual has the help of friends and family, he will probably keep his thought processes to remain in treatment and not surrender. They might most likely give a few hints to the liar.

Tip 4: Determine different diseases

This probably won't be identified with instances of influence. However, one of the main things a specialist has to know when he is looking at the obsessive liars is whether there are other psychological maladjustments. If you can treat different ailments, it might inspire the patient to take a shot at beating the lying condition.

Tip 5: Track any progressions

Following changes in the conduct can let you know whether you are going the correct route with treatment.

Tip 6: Give it time

If the liar is offered the drug to quiet their lying, you should allow it to work before making another assessment. Use instances of influence to do it.

Tip 7: Check their confidence

Ordinarily, the obsessive liar is low in confidence. Building them up and supporting them will give them the inspiration and confidence expected to finish the light.

Tip 8: Determine their past

Knowing instances of influence will enable you to decide why a liar is lying. Some of the time, the liar lies in light of injury and additionally misuse that may have happened when they were more youthful or in the home by and by. This would be a resistance instrument, and in this way, character improvement tips would likely assistance they recuperate alongside advising.

Tip 9: Stay back

As a last resort, avoid the individual. This is presumably the hardest of the systems to finish for yet might be vital.

Tip 10: Depression

The awful thing about the past tip is that the individual may experience the ill effects of melancholy. As you probably are aware of utilizing instances of influence, if so you should attempt to get eh individual to look for assistance for it. Encounters and cutting the individual off may set them over the edge and risk the stinging.

Different Examples of Persuasion Types

Influence is the utilization of systems to change some mind, accepts, activities, or demeanors. There are a few instances of control you may experience.

Many occasions, when somebody can get you to pledge to a thought, you will feel progressively slanted to proceed with it, regardless of whether your unique emotions have changed. This is frequently why somebody will purchase a cake from a bread shop with names incorrectly spelled and the cake a fiasco without remarking on the issue.

Individuals additionally can be convinced by observing others do what is viewed as the social standard. They will, in general, follow other individuals completing a demonstration and feel slanted to duplicate similar practices. This is the reason many teenagers fall unfortunate casualty to companion weight and attempt things they know aren't right.

If somebody is felt to be agreeable, at that point, they are bound to enable themselves to be induced by them. Prime models are legislators and sales rep. Looks and appeal add to the possibility that they are amiable, and individuals frequently tune in to what they need to state many occasions ending up concurring with them.

Power can likewise be a be an extraordinary persuader too. Frequently a specialist figure can cause individuals to get things done, notwithstanding when they realize they are incorrect. Military activities are significant occurrences of this, with a cutting edge model being the Tibetan police activities. Many individuals would be not able to support the personal privileges of the Tibetan individuals, yet the experts in China have induced the military to involve the land.

Instances of influence are not, in every case, terrible. Changing personalities on race and religion can profit many individuals, for example. The craft of power has many aspects and strategies.

Instances of Persuasion - 10 Ways to Focus On Your Objective every Time

Regardless of what the undertaking you will most likely be going after progress. One of the most notable instances of influence is inducing yourself. It very well may be challenging to achieve accomplishment now and again yet it may be done, and with the assistance of these ten positive approaches to center, you can do it. That is the place these instances of influence become possibly an essential factor. When you pursue these tips, what you need is inside reach.

Tip 1: Your reasons are surprising.

When you have a sufficient reason, you can without much of a stretch have the fearlessness to get it going.

Tip 2: Visualizing the target

Perception is simply the point that you can nearly make yourself see your fruitful goals being come to. This will assist you in keeping centered. This is one of the most dominant instances of influence.

Tip 3: Write your goals down.

One of the most significant strides to progress and achieving your goals.

Tip 4: Affirm practical goals.

This will ensure that you induce yourself — an incredible one among the many instances of influence. You can make your very own confirmations by essentially expressing to yourself, "I have now achieved my objective of _____, and have enough fearlessness to hold moving to the following.

Tip 5: Plan of activity.

A game plan is essential to achieving your goals effectively. They can be as straightforward or detailed as you need yet recollect that a necessary arrangement is simpler to recall and work with than an intricate one is.

Tip 6: Measure and track your victories

You can monitor your effectively achieved goals and screen your adventure of intentional living.

Tip 7: Keep a suitable, emotionally supportive network.

Your companion can be extraordinary instances of influence. Everything is continuously more straightforward if you have a companion there to walk the way with you. Merely having somebody there for help, regardless of whether they are not following a similar way as you, can help you a great deal.

Tip 8: Only spotlight on a couple of goals at the time

Concentrating on such a large number of goals will cause pressure and likely some disappointment. This can incredibly harm your self-assurance.

Tip 9: Remain in real life.

Break larger goals down to little ones — for instance, the author. An essayist might need to compose a 5000-word book, possibly on cases of influence, yet can't accomplish it in one day. It is a progressing task spread more than a while as a rule. So littler goals would resemble 2 or 3 pages per day, consistently.

Tip 10: Celebrate.

Probably the best thing on the adventure to conscious living is the demonstration of being useful. Treat yourself and praise your victories.

The Power Of Persuasion Is Within Your Reach

You have to realize that the intensity of influence ought to never be trifled with. It has been utilized during several time by the absolute most dominant and compelling individuals who at any point existed.

You may likewise be shocked to realize that the intensity of influence is something that doesn't require monetary capital or any distinct experience. The fact of the matter is effectively conveying your point, through which you can ideally control others to a similar stage as yours.

What Makes Persuasion Very Effective?

Influence is one of the best methodologies you can use in pretty much every feature of day by day living. You can induce others in promoting, bunch exchanges, and political issues. You can construct connections through the intensity of influence, too.

The critical factor of this type of social impact is that you depend on request as opposed to compelling, which causes individuals to choose for themselves that they need to be in a circumstance in which you can change their perspectives and activities. Individuals like the possibility that they freely settle on choices all alone and to their benefit and influence do that in all respects, viably.

Presuppositions and Goals

Comprehend that all people are wise and balanced. Everybody likewise can learn and build musings, in light of how they see and comprehend their environment. The fundamental objective of influence is to give individuals a chance to need to support and build contemplations as per your very own perspectives.

Correspondence is a fundamental factor in the intensity of influence since one of your destinations is to discover what the other individual is attempting to accomplish.

Through correspondence and model, you will almost certainly rehearse the intensity of influence by creating congruency as far as language, qualities, and convictions. At first, you share data and present essential points of interest that should profit the individual you're attempting to convince. It is conceivable to address several individuals at one time, in this way, coming about to social impact. The intensity of influence develops as more individuals are tended to.

Chapter three
Mentally programming Exposed

Mentally programming method

There are methods for convincing you that are secret, dull, and incredibly compelling. You most likely are accepting mentally conditioning without your insight at this moment. These procedures are the reason you are overweight, smoke, have torment, can't rest, alongside a large portion of your weaknesses.

You have been accepting messages as long as you can remember that have made you question your considerations, convictions, and discernments. This happens continuously, and it has turned into an essential procedure of personal correspondence. These examples of communication frequently are utilized to the advantage of another gathering. Notwithstanding, perceiving these procedures in real life, you can stop them before they hurt you further.

The more significant part of these procedures is viable to the point that the beneficiary energetically reexamines what they see. In any case, these strategies can likewise be powerful emblematically requesting the recipient changes their recognition.

Addressing Brainwashing

One of these secretive mentally programming systems happens inside the configuration of addressing. Continued addressing composed in an unsafe example will make the subject break down things about which they were not by any means thinking. As this procedure continues the subject unknowingly finishes until there is a mess in regards to the first idea or experience. Another memory thought, or adjusted perspective could be the final product.

Here is the thing that happens when talented individual inquiries you. Each time an addressed is presented, you may react with unobtrusive varieties of a story or memory. This gifted professional, sponsor, specialist figure can make you, in the end, question your very own reasoning. The more drawn out this procedure, the more it is rehashed, the less you perceive the example, the more successful the result. Before you know it you don't have the foggiest idea what you think or have encountered and the more you concur with the message, commercial or specialist figures portrayal of the data. You have quite recently been mentally programmed!

Focus and Recognize the Brainwashing

If you focus on the news, to promoters, to power figures, you will begin to see this teaching. A few people are so talented at these strategies that they use it as a standard type of correspondence.

If you are blameless, you will end up being an injured individual. It is fundamentally critical to be wary of these systems. You have to realize that you are under constant attack. When you don't soon, you never again have a unique idea. You will never still have recognizing perspectives. You will never back be accountable for your life. You will figure, you will do, you will buy, you will pursue, and you will be one of the numerous who have been mentally programmed. Furthermore, you won't understand it!

You have to address everything. When you are overweight, when you can't stop smoking, if you are baffled in agony, if you lay conscious around evening time with a sleeping disorder, your cerebrum hustling, keeping you from dozing, in the event that you have any condition wherein another person can profit, that condition was made, and no one but you can switch it.

Mind Control Brainwashing - 3 Common Ways it is Used to Manipulate Others

Mind control mentally programming is a procedure wherein somebody utilizes power and underhanded methods to induce somebody to comply with the desires of the individual in charge. For the most part, this procedure jumps out at the disadvantage of the individual being taught. Other essential names for it incorporate coercive influence, however, change, and thought control, among different titles. There are various manners by which it is typically utilized, and this part will investigate some of them.

One manner by which coercive influence has been utilized is through the approaches of extremist systems around the globe. These systems are not timid at all with regards to applying power to getting what they need, regardless of whether that power is over the top and untrustworthy. In that capacity, they have been known to prevail with regards to teaching their detainees of war with different methods, including consistent, purposeful publicity and torment.

Another way these mind control teaching strategies are utilized is in new religious developments. Regularly new religious gatherings that spring up are driven by incredibly appealing people who employ particularly persuading forces regarding influence, just as the capacity to teach others through different strategies, one of the significant ones being a disconnection from family and companions who aren't individual gathering individuals. By being confined from others with diverse perspectives, you become all the more solidly settled in the gathering's convictions.

The last model is a less evil one, albeit here and there when taken to limits it can prompt terrible outcomes. Individuals from societies and sororities in schools are additionally deceived and made to bear different instances of mental and physical torment and mortification to turn into a piece of the gathering. By obliterating the sense of self through submitting to a more recognizable expert in the group, or through performing different acts that are regularly embarrassing, the individual begins to build up a stable gathering personality and dedication. Frequently, the absurd idea of a portion of the physical tests the hopeful individuals are made to perform can prompt specific real damage, and even passing. This technique for mentally conditioning leads individuals from concrete crews to do things that they would not do, notwithstanding the gathering dynamic driving them forward.

There are numerous instances of mind control teaching other than the three referenced in this part. This is an immense subject that additionally is pertinent to deals, military administration, and numerous different regions. What's more, it is imperative to take note that there are ethical approaches to impact others that don't include any torment or vile mental control.

Mentally conditioning Techniques That They Don't Want You to Know.

Mentally conditioning methods are entirely influential ideas to convince clients or prospects to acknowledge the product offers with no protests effortlessly. It's a typical practice these days for salespeople and system advertisers to get the hang of mentally conditioning procedures to enable them to deal with any business protests better and lift deals. That is for what reason I'm going to impart to you a basic idea regarding this matter can get dramatic changes in your business profession.

One of the indoctrinating systems that I've seen and by and by utilized is the "big and little strategy." Let me clarify it. An individual will at first make an incredibly big offer that naturally gets dismissed by the prospects. When they've rejected the primary offer, the sales reps or system advertisers will make a littler optional offer that is excessively less expensive from the first. When the prospects catch wind of this auxiliary offer, they'll begin to think about the tremendous contrasts that both the offers have and likely pick the littler one.

Give me a chance to give you a model for this procedure. Suppose you're selling two different products at the cost of $400 and $40. Demonstrate your prospects the expensive product first and disclose to them about the advantages that it has. Your, candidates won't be dazzled by the value regardless of how great is the outcome. They won't dismiss the offer legitimately, yet they'll begin to reject it rationally. This is the place you offer the $40 product now and offer a portion of the advantages that it has. The second product that you provided will be considered as a deal, and the prospects will liable to state "YES" to it.

This procedure is a quite incredible mentally programming strategy to convince clients quicker and impact their purchasing choices with the goal that they'll state "YES" rapidly.

Brainwash Yourself for Total Success - A 5-Step Guide

Here are the five steps:

STEP 1 - Get Ready

Go to a region that is tranquil and clean. Ensure there is a pleasant spot to sit. Have a morning timer or clock close-by that is set for 10 minutes. Don't hesitate to fix it for more - the additional time you spend on this, the quicker you will get results.

STEP 2 - Relax

Pause for a moment or two and focus on your relaxing. When any musings come into your psyche, allowed them to pass. If you get diverted, delicately take your consideration back to your breath. When you have a most loved contemplation strategy, don't hesitate to utilize that. The purpose of this step is to loosen up your mind and quiet down your contemplations, so when you feel good using another technique to unwind, use that.

STEP 3 - Visualize Your Success

This is the place the "mentally programming" happens. Picture yourself as totally fruitful. As strikingly as possible, picture what you would do if you were adequate. What might you resemble? Who might you partner yourself with? What might your home resemble? Envision taking a gander at your record balance at the ATM. The more point by point your pictures can get, the better. Envision strolling around each room in your fantasy home. Smell the fragrance originating from your kitchen. What sounds would you hear? Feel the shiny completion on your new vehicle. Feel the sand of your private shoreline filtering through your fingertips. Attempt to utilize the majority of your faculties in your representations. Remember to feel the energy as you picture these things. The more feeling you can deliver, the quicker you will see changes.

STEP 4 - Hold Onto The Feeling

For whatever length of time that you can, clutch the sentiment of being fruitful as you approach your day, attempt to do every one of your assignments through the eyes of a champ. From the outset, the inclination will be gone in a flash. As in anything, particular discipline brings about promising results. After some time, you will most likely clutch this inclination for longer timeframes. It will, likewise end up more grounded and more grounded.

STEP 5 - Rinse and Repeat

This may feel clever or unnatural from the outset, and your subliminal personality may dismiss it. Try not to stress, and you aren't treating it terribly. The more you do these steps, the more familiar the procedure will feel. In the long run, you will be "indoctrinated." What you began simply envisioning yourself to be will be who you presently are. This is the point at which your life will appear to emerge into what you envisioned it to be naturally. Try not to surrender until you have achievement. Every single top entertainer had made progress in their psyches before they at any point accomplished it as a general rule. Should you pick it, this is your destiny as well. Have a fabulous time!

Teach Yourself!

To accurately mentally condition yourself, you may need to see precisely what that way in the first place. This would be the procedure wherein we strip the psyche, not cerebrum, and put in new thoughts, contemplations, and sentiments. Envision an existence where everybody isn't just skilled, however, would like to live on the projects you make for your very own psyche.

Presently to begin this procedure, one would more likely than not comprehend the need to wash your cerebrum or, fundamentally, your brain. As opposed to prevalent thinking, mentally programming can be sheltered, and in many occurrences vital. You can't just eradicate as of now running projects inside your mind. You can't eliminate the motivations that we get by on, for example, relaxing. We don't get up one morning and overlook how to tie our shoes. In any event not without genuine injury to the cerebrum.

What we can do is teach ourselves of thoughts and negative considerations and driving forces. Consequently, we would be left with new emotions and contemplations, which lead to new ideas. To invigorate our programming, you should reboot the framework and reinvent it to do precisely what you need it to do, not what you used to accept. Think about what our identity and what we do, all began with only a thought. Our thoughts originate from the psyche. The psyche is the thing that accumulates our information and projects the mind. The cerebrum is a capacity focus and handling lab for data. The human personality is the thing that uses that data and chooses what we will do with it, be it an antagonistic or constructive decision.

To appropriately comprehend why our mind controls our cerebrum in the way it so picks, one would need to peer inside the present elements of the brain. What do we do? Where do we go? With whom do we partner with? With what beliefs do we direct ourselves? You should comprehend that cerebrum isn't the psyche, and the subconscious isn't the mind. To acknowledge this idea is to start to understand why we do what we do. It is our thoughts and beliefs that guide us. Positive or negative. The mind utilizes what we put in our cerebrum and masterminds it in the subliminal idea. At the point when this is done consistently, our subliminal personality snatches that data and takes it back to the front, the conscious character. This thus is the place our thoughts are made.

Accept you can figure out how to program your psyche to make new thoughts. Would it not be protected to state you can pick whatever life you need. Quite show another experience, fix and make connections more grounded than any you might suspect you have now. It's just coherent to acknowledge that an individual could turn out to be exceedingly rich with mind influence and discover no restrictions.

The regular utilization of the psyche has constrained human cerebrum. In any case, the mind is eternal in its capacity through reality... since you know, you will always remember.

Understanding People - The Best Way to Maximise Sales

In the highly competitive universe of offers, it's regularly very barely noticeable a portion of the more unobtrusive aptitudes of charismatic skill as the strain to distinguish drives, set up gatherings and close arrangements turn into comprehensive. It is the better purposes of being a sales rep, and all the more significant in drawing in with individuals that can prompt more achievement.

The primary center of charisma is the capacity to connect with and influence individuals. Although components, for example, age, cultural foundation, language, and individual character can primarily affect human cooperation, some focal guidelines administer our conduct and which profoundly affect whether we promptly feel good captivating with one another. By getting individuals, you're in a vastly improved position to push the correct catches to make an arrangement more probable. The accompanying provision of tips will assist you with developing an executioner toolbox to compliment your business munitions stockpile and lift your business vocation.

Know Thy Product

Know your items back to front. Having the option to respond to any inquiries on your subject will empower you to manage any cynicism or issues head-on, and sets an unquestionably increasingly expert air. You clients need to become tied up with you before they can get tied up with your item. When you don't have the foggiest idea what you're discussing, you can't fabricate the trust that you have to induce that client further along the business process.

Know the Industry

Stay up to date with industry news, going through 20 minutes or so every morning to get on the ongoing features, and read a couple of news stories. The majority of this should be possible on the web, and only a couple of minutes worth of research each day will give you an advantageous battery of casual discussion points for your specific market. For clients, addressing somebody who has a firm handle on the recent developments in the business is another exhibition of their dedication and excitement to the company, strengthening your situation as an individual from your client's specific gathering and not as an outcast.

Be Personable

People are highly visual, and an attractive individual is instinctually confided in more than they increasingly tousled contender. When meeting customers dress for the event, be adequate, keen and guarantee that you focus on the little subtleties, all of which can help put you beside the challenge and establish an all the more dominant first connection.

It's anything but complicated to attempt to embrace a persona that you figure a customer will like, yet know that bogus personas are exceptionally simple to spot since they are so unnatural. There are standard body language pointers that distinguish If you are lying or being misleading, and embracing a bogus persona will begin setting off these sign. Be friendly, open, and agreeable. Tune in to what your client is letting you know, and utilize that data, later on, to enable correspondence to further. Try not to attempt to be somebody else, yet instead, center around being somebody that the client feels they can converse with.

Give Things Away

Toward the beginning of any business process, clients will usually be watched and doubting, and it's regular human conduct. Having some news stories, the web connects to valuable data or other such assets can indeed exhibit your ability to help your client all in all, not merely in making a deal. The assets ought to be identified with the business that your client works in, yet maybe not crucial to the deal you're attempting to make. Being useful outside of the business process shows that you're after the client's cash, yet in building up a decent expert relationship.

Go That Extra Mile

When going to a gathering, do some additional examination to discover somewhat more about your client or their organization. This will enable you to stand out among the challenge and can allow a client to feel progressively esteemed.

Answer all brings in the timeliest design conceivable and convey on any guarantees that you make to a client. This is the best trust-building device that you have. A client can't purchase from somebody they don't trust. Building trust is the establishment of any continuous relationship, and beginning a business relationship off with a high level of confidence will expand progressing deals later, so going the additional mile will satisfy.

Utilize the Right Language

All sales reps are educated to utilize open-finished inquiries to prop a discussion up, one of the essential correspondence standards. What's more, using the correct words and being aware of your body language will be vital in building up an affinity with a potential client. Regularly over 55% of your correspondence is non-verbal, imparted through your body pose. Receiving a non-undermining, open body language is vital to making your client feel good in your quality. When the client doesn't feel right, at that point, they won't confide in you. If they don't confide in you, they won't purchase from you.

Utilizing the correct words will likewise assist you with taking alternate routes into a client's mind. Using a similar phrasing as your client is utilizing can position you as a significant aspect of a gathering, one of the pack. Utilizing the correct wording demonstrates that you comprehend your client and are not a pariah.

Old fashioned is Best School.

With regards to human collaboration, vis-à-vis or vocal correspondence is as yet the most flawlessly awesome structure. This doesn't imply that there's the wrong spot for email or even web-based life in the realm of offers. However, innovation ought to be a technique for you to oversee and source your clients. With regards to the last stages, utilize the telephone, and organize vis-à-vis gatherings.

Human Schedules

Invest energy to see how your clients structure their day. Are there clear focuses during which a telephone call from you would be increasingly welcome? Is sending an email at a specific time liable to end in it being erased or even plain disregarded because you've sent it at the pinnacle movement time?

See how your clients plan they are everyday exercises and plan your day around this. Try not to call clients when they're probably going to be at their busiest, and don't prospect for new leads when your present points are all the more ready and ready to accept a call from you!

NLP

Contemplating the nuts and bolts of NLP, or Neuro-Linguistic Programming, can assist you with making your correspondence with clients unquestionably progressively viable by giving you an understanding into the sort of individual your client is and how to best structure your words and sentences to make your messages increasingly worthy to that client. Study NLP and grasp entirely what it offers.

How to Read People's Minds - The Secret Tricks to Read People's Thoughts

Probably the greatest puzzle of humanity is finding the key to how to peruse individuals' brains. When you could examine individuals' contemplations, you could know precisely what someone else is thinking. The intensity of mind perusing traps and methods truly lies in your capacity by the way you are reading the conduct and flag that the other individual gives you. Here are the mystery approaches to understand individuals' musings through non-verbal communication. When you recognize what an individual is supposing, you are in control of fantastic information that can enable you to lead cooperation to support you.

Perusing non-verbal communication is fun and straightforward. A large portion of us doesn't do this deliberately, so we neglect to perceive precisely what an incredible personality perusing procedure it is. Here are a few things to watch out for to kick you off:

- If they are confronting you, they are tuning in and focusing on you. In any case, if they are dismissed, they are not centered on you. When they are shaking side to side, they are anxious and need to end the conversation. A turned back is an indication of purposely overlooking or staying away from somebody.

- When somebody backs up, on an intuitive level, they feel undermined and are withdrawing from you. If somebody is step by step moving towards you, they are keen on you or what you are stating.

- Pointing their knees or their feet towards you is a widespread consent to they are in arrangement with you, they are adjusting their stance to yours.

- If they start to imitate your non-verbal communication, that is an indication that you are driving the discussion.

- Crossed arms are an indication of preventiveness or disdain, the particular case is the point at which the thumbs are unmistakably visible and pointing upwards, that implies they are feeling disconnected yet friendly.

- If their hands are confronting you with open palms, at that point they are accessible/responsive to what you are stating.

- If eyes look upward to one side, they are attempting to make a picture from nothing. They are effectively utilizing their creative mind, and this can be an indication that they are making up whatever they are disclosing to you. If their eyes look upwards to one side, they are attempting to recall a specific picture, get to a particular memory. These are only the typical rules, a few people, particularly the left-gave, have the contrary eye developments, so it's essential to get a standard perusing by convincing them to recollect something that you know occurred

A large portion of these things we will feel during our collaborations. Without giving mindful consideration, we will begin to sense when an individual is getting to be cautious and at precisely that point see their shut non-verbal communication. Figuring out how to focus on your sentiments is a simple method to begin ending up progressively mindful of what the non-verbal communication of others is letting you know.

Beside sociopaths and constant liars, double-dealing is distressing. When we are worried, blood flow is organized to the essential organs and occupied away from the limits. If somebody is lying, they are in all respects prone to have cold hands. This pressure will likewise make the individual progressively anxious because of a loud clamor or some other alarm. In any case, recollect, stress does not suggest trickery.

Eye contact when we are lying isn't frequent. However, it very well may be constrained. When an individual begins looking that feels off, at that point, they are presumably angling something obscure.

How an individual is thinking will be reflected in the words they use and the inquiries they pose. Somebody who likes to discuss social circumstances and connections is somebody who is centered around relational connections and will react much better to associations that consolidate those components. Relationships depend on feelings, and these individuals will be influenced more by enthusiastic contentions than legitimate ones.

By focusing on every one of the signs an individual is accidentally radiating, you will appear to peruse their brain. These methods will give you a familiarity with what others are feeling that you may even begin to astonish yourself with your precision. The vast majority are so centered around what they are going to state straightaway or what they look for from communication that they are just redirecting an exceptionally modest quantity of their thoughtfulness regarding the other individual. When we center our complete consideration around what the other individual is doing and saying, we increase enormous understanding into what they are thinking, however, how they believe.

Step by step instructions to Read People Like A Book

Find how to peruse individuals like a book, and you will most likely accomplish quite a lot more with other individuals. When you comprehend what is happening within them, at that point, you can impact, induce, and even personality control them.

How you do that is by figuring out how to perceive particular character examples and manners by which they structure their inside experience.

For instance, you can distinguish whether somebody is an individual who can deal with weight well and can keep his cool even in pressure circumstances.

There are three principal ways for how individuals react to pressure: enthusiastic, picking, or thinking. Passionate individuals are the individuals who get tossed into specific sentiments and after that can do nothing about it. Picking individuals are the individuals who at first experience the sentiments, yet then they choose to remove themselves from them and work things through sensibly. And afterward, there are the individuals who don't react genuinely by any stretch of the imagination - they act judiciously, legitimately, and thoroughly consider things immediately.

One way you can do this is to get some information about a work circumstance where they experienced inconvenience. Enthusiastic individuals will remember the experience somewhat - you can hear the feelings in their manner of speaking, you can perceive how the muscles in their face worry, their body stance or signals may change.

For decision individuals, you may at first observe that however, then they go again into the unbiased state.

Furthermore, "scholars" won't go into feelings by any means and discuss the actualities.

Presently when you read this, it may appear as though scholars are the best sort to be in, yet it indeed relies on what kind of circumstance. For instance, a considerable lot of the world's best cooks will, in general, be passionate individuals - and that is no fortuitous event because to be excellent in their profession, they have to feel, sense and experience things.

In any case, a specialist ought not to be an exceptionally enthusiastic individual, but instead a scholar.

What's more, with regards to directing occupations or positions where relational aptitudes are required, at that point "choosers" are regularly best, since they can sincerely react to someone else's worry, yet they can likewise observe the reasonable side of it.

So when you are in a high-stress circumstance, for instance, you could help a passionate individual by saying: "Would you be able to envision how we'll feel about this circumstance quite a while from now, when we think back on this?"

This causes them to disassociate themselves from the circumstance.

Contingent on what sort of individual you are conversing with, various methodologies will generally work viably. Likewise, when you need to persuade enthusiastic individuals, utilize enthusiastic words, that get them energetic. Use words like "amazing", "intense", "unprecedented".

For "choosers," you can utilize expressions like: "This isn't simply energizing and fun, it additionally bodes well." And for "masterminds," you present the hard certainties. Notice statistics, talk about "unwavering discernment" and "the cool reality."

As should be obvious, it takes some training to figure out how to peruse individuals like a book - yet once you become acquainted with this, you can without much of a stretch utilize this information to control other individuals.

Personality Psychology

Personality brain science is the investigation of individual contrasts in conduct and thinking. We consider individuals having remarkable characters, and we have words to portray them-your companion is decent, your instructor is mean, your more youthful sibling is timid, etc. When you dive further into personality, it's much more intricate than single word characteristics or even a few attributes set up together. Your companion is decent to you, however, would she say she is pleasant to her most noticeably awful foe? Your instructor is mean, yet how can he act with his better half and youngsters? Your more youthful sibling is bashful; however, how can he work inside the home and within sight of just your family? Our characters can change contingent upon the circumstance we're in. However, it appears there must be some temperament, or center, or some essential property that separates individuals from others. So what precisely establishes personality? This is the thing that personality brain research attempts to dissect, find, and clarify.

Above all else, personality needs to originate from someplace. Nature is thought of something individuals are brought into the world with, something that is "them" and their identity. Surely, personality is exceedingly hereditary you may wind up displaying similar personality qualities and quirks as your folks, and indistinguishable twins have been appeared to show fundamentally the same as miens. Science can help clarify how individuals think and act, yet others would differ about this being the entire picture. Natural impacts and the decisions we make can likewise bigly affect our characters. A lively tyke may encounter injury and develop to be shy as a grown-up, or he may defeat struggle and grow up to be versatile. Nature, support and through and through freedom all connect and it's this interchange seems to shape personality.

The most present hypothesis in personality brain research is the "if...then" profile. It clarifies personality through this model-if an individual is in this circumstance, it enacts specific musings and sentiments, making the individual demonstration in that manner. Everyone has an inside model that comprises of what is designated "psychological full of feeling units." They are organized with the goal that an outside occasion initiates individual units, which actuate others, etc. in a chain until it prompts an activity. The intellectual, emotional unit structures we have created rely upon our natural temperament, culture, and circumstance.

The "if...then" profile is an inventive and pervasive model of personality. However, science is an endless procedure, and this model will undoubtedly be adjusted later on. Imagine a scenario in which "if...then" profiles themselves change. This will be tended to with a more up to date model, and more up to date models will pursue.

Chapter four

How to Manipulate Others - Using Underground Hypnosis Techniques

Many individuals are searching for ways on the best way to control others, as they understand that they can accomplish what they need in life effectively when individuals around them are tuning in to them. Is it accurate to say that it isn't decent when individuals are adhering to your guidelines whatever you request that they do? Affecting and controlling individuals isn't a simple aptitude to ace. It needs learning and steady practices to achieve the level whereby you can control any individuals you need.

Hypnotizing others is to place them in a perspective whereby they are defenseless against your 'direction'. 'Words' are utilized to speak with their inconspicuous personalities, and they are unconscious of themselves being entranced. You won't almost certainly control them. Up to a specific level, you can control them by making a verbal recommendation to their subliminal personalities.

Underground entrancing techniques enable you to utilize trigger expressions and words to put your objectives in a stupor state, consequently permitting your 'directions' to sneak through and enter their subliminal personalities. You will likewise figure out how to peruse the non-verbal communication of your objectives and state various expressions or words as indicated by the developments and signals they make.

A great many people use trance techniques to accomplish the accompanying:

1. Draw in and allure the contrary sex, or getting the opposite sex to begin to look all starry eyed at them.

2. Addition compatibility with individuals and win fellowships, making other individuals to like them.

3. Get individuals to purchase items or administrations from them.

4. Get others to do whatever other things that will profit themselves.

Manipulation Techniques

We had taken in the craft of control as far back as when we were newborn children. At the point when an infant cries when her mother puts her to bed is one method for power to get their direction. Power is in the very center of each human. With the immense information, we have aggregated until nowadays and with the consistently developing innovation that makes data simple to get to, learning the capacity to persuade others is inside handle.

Controlling Techniques these days prove to be useful with the ascent of the web. Numerous individuals can investigate and think about the sentiments and encounters of the general population around the globe. Getting the hang of controlling strategies do build your public self. Information and relational abilities, which is a significant fixing in our connection and human relationship, can carry accomplishment to an individual. For individuals who are claiming to know the expertise, yet don't generally realize how to actualize it, will begin ineffectively. Along these lines, understanding the fundamentals of what can represent the deciding moment your methodology is a significant procedure, to start with.

Numerous systems are utilized with regards to control. A couple of messy traps are being used by individuals to control others. Although consequently, they would likewise stumble into the hardship of getting similar karma they deliberately practice.

There are a couple of control procedures that don't include guileful or beguiling motions. Control methods are utilized for the most part to exceed the process of others yet, at the same time, using the objectives and principles of reasonable challenge. In business, we have to out-think our rivals by giving the best enthusiasm to our customers and noting the requirements of our clients. We can stay aware of our opposition by moving ourselves to accomplish more and by getting bolster that we need in connection to personal growth.

We should know that control includes mind collaboration since we can persuade an individual when we read his or her brain.

In a natural way of life don't act just as predators we are additionally prey for other people. Therefore, we have to realize that "Not all facts are truly valid." Individuals will, in general, have faith in things regardless of whether they are made to accept that it is valid. At the point when a sales rep is selling their item, they would cause you to take that it is valuable. We have to comprehend that they are just utilizing control strategies to get us in their manner.

We likewise need to comprehend that "Being impeccable is a difficulty." Everyone intends to be impeccable and would effectively change such flaws. Now and then we can redesign or improve something yet these progressions areas, however not flawlessly done. A brightening cream doesn't generally give you the ideal white skin that you need to accomplish if you doesn't usually have a white composition. Control strategies possibly work longer when they depend on the real world.

Mind Control - 4 Tips for Becoming Master Manipulator

You can exercise mind control on indeed every individual. The facts demonstrate that a few people have substantial cognizant obstruction. However, this does not imply that they can't be affected. All you need to do to turn into an ace controller is to have the correct information, apparatuses, and outlook.

Utilize the accompanying exhortation to learn and prepare mind control strategies and aptitudes. You will positively begin getting results soon.

Understand the maximum capacity of the power mind.

The facts demonstrate that some strategy for control work dependent on the utilization of power and the encountering of dread. In any case, there are considerably more viable approaches to impact individuals and their psyche, specifically.

The term power mind, by and large, alludes to the self-control we as a whole have. This self-discipline is driven by our subliminal personality and, specifically, by out convictions, feelings and wants, which all have a place with it. Consider it, and we feel persuaded and roused to get things done. We are not learning these.

Your errand as a mind control professional is to misuse these subliminal powers to impact the power mind. When you implant the thought into the individual's head, he will and amazingly propelled to do it.

Utilize undercover mesmerizing for mind control.

There is plenty of systems for control that you can apply. These range from blackmail to love besieging. In any case, undercover mesmerizing is substantially more subtle and successful than every one of them.

Undercover entrancing, otherwise called conversational trance, is a sort of trancelike impact that you practice during a discussion. This strategy is utilized for impacting the subliminal personality directly. Thus, the mighty brain of the individual is completely misused.

The individual does not understand that he is spellbound. You are setting him up for making your subliminal order by driving him to a fanciful circumstance or potentially state of mind.

At that point, you instruct him. This order is a natural continuation of the circumstance or potentially disposition that you have set up for the individual.

All in all, deep trance is a psychological methodology for mind control that requires preparing.

You need to figure out how to assemble affinity with the individual you need to enter. You need to figure out how to open the individual's intuitive personality utilizing his creative mind. You need to figure out how to make inserted directions directly.

Gain trust in yourself and your abilities as a controller.

Regardless of the mind control technique, you are utilizing; you must be sure about what you are doing. An individual without high confidence will feel anxious or uncertain about his activities. This can prompt disappointment.

It is essential for you to gain self-assurance, as you learn more understanding. You ought to have a precise thought of how incredible you are a controller. All the more important, you ought not to focus on individuals and components that are harming your confidence.

The best controllers are iron men. They generally remain in control. Other individuals' feelings and assessments never influence them. They are centered constantly. They are utilizing their capacity mind's capability to stay sure and to succeed.

Play subtle psychological traps with individuals' minds.

This is fundamental for applying clandestine entrancing and other successful personality control strategies. These little traps can enable you to get somebody defenseless to control. They can be utilized for positive control also.

It is amazingly simple to win an individual's trust and offer to him, When you share a secret, for example. This demonstrates you confide in this individual, so thus, he will confide in you. Also, you don't impart important secret things to individuals that you don't care for. Since the individual feels that you like him, he begins enjoying you also.

Not every psychological trap for control are that straightforward. Now and then you may need to utilize progressively sophisticated techniques for achieving the subliminal personality, for example, design interferes.

These procedures, which range from an abrupt and sudden snicker to a posing an awkward inquiry, can without much of a stretch get any individual into a condition of a daze. The structure then on, he is yours to control.

You have recently figured out how to turn into an ace at the top of the priority list control. Continue adapting more to turn into a far better controller.

The Art of Manipulation - Using Emotions to Manipulate People

If you need to control individuals sincerely, at that point, you have to consider yourself a craftsman who skillfully plays out his specialty that the watchers of the artistry are just ready to see the final product and not comprehend the complexities of his functions.

You realize that you are going out on a limb by attempting to control others so; the key here is to fly under the radar and abstain from getting captured. When you are figuring out how to manage others, do it gradually beginning with your companions and close family. Along these lines of rehearsing can be contrasted with a military craftsman rehearsing informal sparring before he takes on genuine adversaries.

Presently, that you realize how to begin, we will examine what to do to control individuals effectively. In particular, we will perceive how to utilize the overwhelming feelings of individuals to get what we need. The prevailing feeling shifts from individual to individual. For example, an individual who is keen on financial exchanges, horse hustling, or Forex will capitulate to traps that focus on the insatiability factor. Then again, an individual intrigued by philanthropy, generosity, or church will be available to any recommendations that give him a 'vibe decent' impact.

When you know the predominant feeling of the individual, then you can tailor your words and activities that intrigue to the prevailing attitude of the individual.

From the start, you will think that it is hard to make sense of this; however, as you watch their examples of conduct, you can 'figure out the code' in a couple of days.

The fascinating thing is once you begin doing this, you will make a lot of 'character profiles' in your mind that the time taken to break the code will continue diminishing each time until you achieve a phase where you will almost certainly spot designs in an individual's conduct inside a couple of minutes.

At last, we will perceive what sort of disposition is required to learn compelling control. What you are going to peruse is somewhat substantial; however, after all, power is certifiably not a light subject so focus. You have to consider yourself a researcher, and the world is your lab, and people resemble the rodents in your lab. A researcher infuses various mixes on rodent and watches its conduct and after that, records the outcomes. In like manner, you have to continually figure out how individuals react to various upgrade and record the perceptions in your brain for last use.

The most effective method to Manipulate People and Get Them to Do Anything You Want Them to Do

Have you at any point thought of how to control individuals and get them to do whatever you need them to do? If this at any point came into your brain, at that point, there is one correspondence expertise that you need to realize, that is conversational entrancing.

This is a correspondence aptitude that given you a chance to mesmerize somebody through an easygoing discussion. It's anything but a troublesome ability to ace; what you will do is basically to speak with the subliminal personality of the individual you are conversing with.

There are three principal strategies that you have to ace to entrance somebody through conversational spellbinding.

1) Using Your Body Language - You can impact others' reasoning and observations by utilizing your non-verbal communication. There are some non-verbal communication signs that you can use to make somebody feel unwind and agreeable around you.

2) Create Rapport - You can make decent compatibility and "interface' with somebody and cause them to turn out to be progressively open and OK with you. Making high affinity is pivotal before you need to spellbind somebody and to get them to pursue your directions.

Reflecting is one of the systems that you can use to gain affinity with somebody. For instance, talking in the same traits from different people can make an 'enjoying' from them as individuals will, in general, like individuals who are such as themselves.

3) Hypnotic Language - This is the most dominant part during the time spent mesmerize somebody. Sleep inducing language can be as spoken and composed; the principle motivation behind utilizing it is to change an individual's feelings and brain in a split second.

Utilizing entrancing language is the answer to "how to control individuals." By using specific strategies, individuals are being pulled in and concentrated on your discourse (or written words) which has concealed directions in it. Their intuitive personality will tune in to your instructions, and they will do anything you desire them to do.

How to Mind Control Someone - 5 Psychological Tactics Used to Control Our Actions

Examining how to mind control somebody can be a disputable point because of the many negative ways mind control has been used is as yet being used right up 'til the present time. Governments around the globe, particularly the authoritarian assortment, use mentally conditioning strategies and thought control against detainees of war and other criminal components to bond their hang on power and curb incendiary elements in their social orders. Religious sects use mind control to reinforce their grasp on the minds of followers. Once in a while, the techniques for control are physical, including different strategies for the torment that after some time, affect the mind of an individual.

Furthermore, on various occasions, the procedure is mental, including a direct mental assault on the individual to get them to change their perspectives or conduct. This part will manage five usual ways. However, control is used to control the activities of individuals.

There are numerous strategies that somebody needs to realize how to mind control somebody can learn and rehearse. Not these strategies are demonstrated ones so you should attempt them to perceive what works best for you. You should know that a portion of these strategies genuinely isn't in all great conscience morally stable.

1) Hypnosis is a deep-rooted technique used to actuate a trancelike stupor, wherein recommendations are made to the subject's subliminal mind. Once in a stupor, an individual winds up easily affected to proposals, and this can have the impact of mind control in the emotional changes that can happen in an individual's conduct and mindset.

2) Another technique is well known in religious cliques. In such a case, an individual may give the majority of their ordinary riches and advantages for the

development, winding up reliant on the gathering and its pioneer. With all associations with the past cut off, the individual is a straightforward subject for mind control, as the majority of their expectations, dreams, and connections are joined to the gathering.

3) A high weight barrage of complicated addresses that empower daze acknowledgment of specific standards, values, standards, principles, dismissing intelligent intuition en route, is another technique.

4) A constant flood of verbal abuse can separate the most grounded safeguards and pulverize the hardest soul, prompting robust control of an individual's mind.

5) moreover, unchanging principles like what we find in prisons today are another technique. In such places, mealtimes, showers, exercise times, and lockdowns are altogether fixed, and authorization is required for everything. These basic standards can confuse an individual and make them mentally ward to the degree that it turns out to be anything but difficult to embed thought control.

Figuring out how to mind control somebody is a substantial undertaking, and it ought to be paid attention to very by the individuals who need to stroll down that street. Full oversight over someone else is quite often deceptive, yet there is nothing amiss with utilizing strategies to convince others. The key is to have some ethical benchmarks to abstain from exploiting individuals.

How to Use Mind Manipulation Techniques to Make a Woman Feel Emotionally Addicted to You - Quickly!

There is consistently a man out there who can challenge the standard that states just incredible looking men can get the ladies, and the ugly men need to live with their moms until they are old and undesirable. That one ugly person will, in any case, have accomplishment with any lady based on his personal preference. You more likely than not stood amazed in any event once how he does this.

In the first place, that man realizes that his looks are not significant. In actuality, not being attractive can support a man. Usually, such men are so used to dismissal that they don't even sincerely enlist their looks any longer since they don't consider what they could lose.

Since you are as of now in the correct mentality, you would now be able to chip away at a few different things. Most importantly, you can bring the lady that you need down from the platform you have left her on. All in all, ladies are utilized to men pursuing them and yearning for them, so it isn't surprising if men who unexpectedly treat them - routinely, even - will genuinely stick out. When you can demonstrate that sort of an easygoing frame of mind and demonstrate that her looks genuinely aren't that significant, she will be considerably more inspired by what you bring to the table than what other men bring to the table.

In the wake of achieving this, it would be high time for you to get inside her head and discover what you could do about it. Female personalities happen to be frightening and dangerous spots, so controlling them can be very troublesome. Nonetheless, mesmerizing can take care of business. Doing this will give you a proportion of security since you will know her activities and have the option to discover her best courses of action. Just by knowing which sentiments to trigger, you can avoid different responses at some random time.

Mind Manipulation Techniques - How to Protect Yourself From Mind Manipulation Techniques

Mind manipulation procedures are not just prevalent on TV appears or in films. Many people today utilize mind manipulation strategies to compel a person to accomplish something without wanting to.

With the end goal for you to abstain from being constrained by these mind manipulation procedures, you have to know the manners in which that an individual can get into your brain and controlling you to pick up the preferred position.

Here are some mind manipulation systems that you should think about going to abstain from being constrained by it.

Not All Truths Are True

Much of the time, people will regularly believe it's actually if they are made to accept that it is. This technique is utilized by deals operators forcing other people to purchase their item, regardless of whether it doesn't generally profit them that much.

To have the option to maintain a strategic distance from mind manipulation methods of this sort, don't accept their words as irrefutable truth. Flavor it up with a smidgen of uncertainty that will lead you to scrutinize the validity and reliability of their cases.

A few people have the endowment of persuading people that what they're stating is the single thing that is valid. Be alert. Do your due determination and research on their experience and other people's surveys.

Being Perfect Is An Impossibility

You have to understand that we are flawed creatures, and no item and human-related activities can transform us into an ideal man.

You ought to acknowledge there are specific kinds of mind manipulation systems that go after those people that are very uncertain about their capacities, and even the individuals who are experiencing their defect - or so they are persuaded.

A genuine case of this is TV advertisements that state being reasonable cleaned is lovely and is the best way to excellence.

Dreams Are Considered As Nothing

One of the more typical personality manipulation methods being utilized by con artists and fraudsters today is giving their activities an "otherworldly" vibe.

Many people today are very keen on the idea of enchantment and supernatural quality, and a few people utilize this pandemic interest to drive a person to perform something that will not the slightest bit produce the health outcomes. To ensure yourself, don't be excessively effectively astounded by "enchantment." Applaud it, however, don't accept it as reality.

Chapter five
How To Get Anything You Want

Achievement, just characterized, implies getting anything you desire. However shortsighted that definition might be, the vast majority would concur that an individual who is useful in a specific field or region is so on the grounds that the person in question has figured out how to accomplish something explicit, and that something precise is an objective or item which the individual had been needing or wanting for before his or her achieving it.

Before we discover how to get anything you need throughout everyday life, we should initially get practical.

What is a portion of the things which we may need yet we genuinely and sincerely realize that we will never under any circumstance get? When you have that rundown of tricky, unachievable stuff in your mind and dispense with them, we may continue.

A few models may include: flying noticeable all around by fluttering your arms, cause a pink mammoth to appear out of nowhere, taking in space, squaring a circle, and so forth.

Presently what is those things which you've wanted continuously at this point have never come around to attempt to achieve? These are things which you know are feasible for you, with a considerable measure of exertion on your part, yet something is keeping you away from accomplishing them, either intentionally or unknowingly, purposely or not.

With the goal for you to get anything you need throughout everyday life, you should settle on the levelheaded choice to solidly characterize what you need and need. It is worthless over the long haul if you continue getting things out of your impulses and imprudent wants as opposed to out of what you need to push you ahead throughout everyday life, in whatever unique circumstance and how you characterize that for yourself.

You can start by asking yourself a couple of hard-hitting, legit inquiries regarding the course your life is going and your real inspirations for craving what you look to have.

What do I need?

For what reason do I need it?

What are my real inspirations for needing it?

What are the valid purposes behind requiring it?

What will I see after I've got it?

What will I experience after I've accomplished it?

What will change after I've accomplished it? What won't change?

Who or what will I become after I've obtained it?

In what capacity will it influence the others around me?

Truly this: getting what you need is very simple. It is as of now transpiring 24 hours per day, seven days, 365 days a year. In any case, it is the choice to characterize what you need that is hard for a great many people.

That prohibits the real procedure of approaching achieving what you need, the anticipation, avoidance or defeating of snags that ruin you from getting what you need and after that keeping what you need once you've got it. A few things which you work for will evade your grip if you don't do certain things to ensure they remain with you.

This is called the upkeep.

Since I've given you a brutal and genuinely necessary rude awakening on what you need to get, let me address the essential components or fixings that go into making up the way toward getting what you need.

1. An unmistakable mental impression of your objective. You as of now have this, ideally, if you've asked yourself those inquiries recommended above adequately and savagely. It is much improved if your mental impression emerges as a composed paper expressing your objective or a real visual picture of

your objective (photos, pictures, illustrations, and so on).

2. A solid well-ordered game plan to get towards your objective. This activity plan has probably been utilized by another person to accomplish the equivalent or comparative thing to what you presently need, which means, it more likely than not been demonstrated to work. It must be duplicable, for example, anybody on Earth with similar assets accessible must almost certainly accomplish something very similar.

3. Activity. Things won't move without anyone else to work for you until you move them yourself, except if another person drives them. The vast majority come up short at this stage either because of an absence of inspiration to proceed onward after experiencing a minor or fair misfortune. Or then again they neglect to begin by any means - the issue of hesitation.

It's just as simple as that Target, Plan, Action. We need not go into the minute technical subtleties of every single component in this formula for progress as they are generally merely that - technicalities - which you will most likely discover in increasingly intensive objective setting reading the material, courses, and materials.

Prosperity - How to Get Anything You Want This Year Using Scientific Principles

When you are genuinely attempting to turn your life around this year, at that point, look no further. Utilizing the demonstrated Science of Quantum Abundance, you can change your family tree. Using merely the intensity of your subliminal and definite activity, you can figure out how to get anything you truly desire. Peruse on to discover how you never again need to endure a lot of new-age ballyhoos to end up useful.

The Science of Quantum Abundance is the basic rule that your world turns into the entirety of the things that you consider the most in your intuitive personality. Consider it for a second. If you think another vehicle always, in the long run, you will meander over to the vendor and get one. Regardless of whether it makes you a year to make a move, the picture in your brain is extraordinary to the point that you can't stand it any longer and you will have that vehicle.

You can figure out how to utilize this rule to coordinate how your very own life will wind up. Regardless of whether you are searching for progress, something little and substantial, or another experience for your family, the intensity of your intuitive personality will demonstrate to you the way.

To begin with, you should figure out how to clear your brain of the negative considerations that are holding you down. The universe works in positive explanations. Therefore when you expect that you will have a terrible encounter and that is all you consider, at that point, you will be allowed an awful contact. That will be all that your mind will see, and that will be all that you will follow up on.

Then again, consider how incredible this could be for the general population that can concentrate their musings on the things that they DO need. This is the place the Science of Quantum Abundance becomes an integral factor. You will figure out how to evacuate a significant number of the negative musings that are keeping you stuck in your present position and supplant them with positive considerations that work towards your objective. You subliminal personality murmurs along out of sight, taking care of these complicated issues for you, without you notwithstanding thinking about it. At the point when enlightens come up the world that will enable you to get to where you need to go, your mind will give you a sign that you have to follow up on it.

Activity is the way to this entire procedure. This isn't something where you can sit at home and wish for a superior life. You need to follow up on it. When you can roll out these improvements, the world will be at your feet, and anything you need will be conceivable. You just genuinely should need it all together for the framework to work.

How To Get Anything You Want In Life Using Law Of Attraction

Choose WHAT YOU WANT. Consider it. Envision that you have no constraints at all. Envision that you can be, do or have anything you need throughout everyday life (really you do). Think about an ideal world where you are a perfect rendition of you (really you do now). Have no dread about it. What's more, when you feel dread, it isn't so terrible, because that is the beginning stage. That is disclosing to you that you are concentrating on the things you don't need. Presently, you can focus on inverse and... Bingo! Currently, you recognize what you need throughout everyday life.

Record IT WITH DETAILS. After you recognize what is that you wish to be, do, or have throughout everyday life, you have to make the following stride: Write down it, precisely how you need it when you need it. How you need. Make sure to don't hesitate to inquire. It resembles you having a no-restriction credit card, with a Universal index that contains everything that you can envision. Feel excited, forgetting it. It's imperative to compose it in the current state. As you previously have it.

Envision YOURSELF HAVING, DOING OR BEING WHAT YOU WANT before you begin your day. Directly after you open your eyes in the first part of the day, put aside a couple of minutes, somewhere in the range of 5 and 20, to be alone, and calm. Seat comfortably, breath profound and get your list of things to get, and wish after wish, understanding one cove one, and close your eyes and envision yourself as previously having those things. Utilize every one of your faculties. Heads up, hear it, smell it, believe it. It's your time, and the main thing isolating those things from you is your psyche. Feel the delight of having all that you merit by celestial equity. Regardless of where you live. Irrespective of the administration you have. Regardless of the economy. Regardless of the earth. We as a whole, life in the Universe, and these are its laws. If you can think it and can feel thankful and upbeat of having it, it will show.

Follow up on IT WITH INSPIRATION — everyday checks. I realize you figure you don't have time. I know you think you don't have money. I know you figure you don't have the training. I know you figure you don't have the associations... Nor was I, nor every man or lady who have prevailing ridiculous. The significant thing is to begin acting. Attempt to do, every day, one thing that gets you closer to your desires. Anything. There's no such thing as too little activity. Anything will help. If you begin acting with whatever you have or any place you are, the Universe will manage you and will demonstrate your new instruments, individuals, conditions, and everything you have to get to the pot of gold.

Provide for THE WORLD WHATEVER YOU WANT BACK. As the law of fascination says: Likes draws in like. The act of circumstances and logical results: Anything you offer out to the Universe, you'll turn the tables on least in ten times return. So when you need money, give money, if you need love, give love, when you need openings, provide for someone else. Significantly, you deliver those things with affection. With the goal of giving, not getting. In case you're not recognizable to offer since you figure you will have less, attempt it, and gradually it will feel much improved and better. Furthermore, your reality will change. I guarantee.

Segregate FROM IT. This is where individuals, including my instructors and myself, have the hardest time getting it. It is more significant than the majority of the previous. After you did everything I pointed, you have to separate from the outcome. You have to trust it's en route to meet you. You need to believe that when it hasn't arrived, this is because you're not yet prepared to be, do or have that thing. Get your work done, however without connection. The Universe will hugely compensate you if you spread this progression.

BE HAPPY AND FEEL GOOD ALL THE TIME. For what reason do you think we are here? Indeed, truth is stranger than fiction. To be cheerful. Honestly, to learn, yes to see a few things, yes to help other people, yes to cherish. Those things will be when you appreciate every minute in your life, and be cheerful what's more, in reverse. Truly! That is it!

Straightforward, huh? Every one of the things you need throughout everyday life, you need them since you figure those things will satisfy you. The world doesn't work that way. You should be upbeat first, and after that everything you need will show. You needn't bother with affection, money, a great car, companions, to be cheerful. You need to bargain for yourself to be glad. Regardless. You can generally concentrate on the things that are going on decent, and you will feel upbeat. And after that, the Universe will give the stuff you pull in. The things that fulfill you and feeling better. Loads of them. You have to create that feeling first. The most significant thing in your life is to feel better. At that point, everything will fix itself.

How to Get What You Want - Seriously?

It doesn't make a difference if you are five years of age or you are 50 years of age. We, as a whole, need various things. For instance, the multi-year old may need another action figure for Christmas. The multi-year old needs to get back fit as a fiddle. Through this part, we will allude again to the two models and call attention to a considerable differentiation.

I am getting what you need when you're youthful.

Keep in mind when you were a tyke, and you needed something? What is standing out to prevent you from getting it? Nothing! Sure your mom or father may have interceded on specific events, yet practically there was nothing that was going to remain in your manner. Youngsters are extraordinary because they don't have the foggiest idea about the word unimaginable. They don't have the foggiest idea about the word can't. Their imagination permits them to discover an answer, and in the long run, get whatever it is they need.

Shouldn't something is said about when you get more seasoned?

This is the place a noteworthy issue comes in. Why don't such a significant number of grown-ups have what they need? It is a result of our programming and outside impact from our condition. The more established you get, you will always hear things like:

- "try not to do that."
- "that is off-base."
- "that is not appropriate."
- "You can't do that."

- "find a genuine line of work."
- "get genuine."
- "lift your hand."
- "sit upright."

The rundown continues forever. There is a psychological pen around us, and it gets littler the more seasoned we get. Society and our capricious culture have given us a 'can't do' disposition while endeavoring to acclimate us. You can see it in government-funded schools, holy places and everywhere throughout the news.

The multi-year old will figure out how to get that frozen treat, while the multi-year keeps on working at an occupation he hates because he supposes he can't do whatever else.

What is the arrangement?

Free your psyche. You can have completely anything you want in this life. When you let other individuals make your deduction for you, you will get no opportunity at all. It is exceptionally hard for a few, however, in light of the numerous long periods of outside impact.

You should acknowledge you can change how you think. When you do that, you will have no issue getting what you need. Your entire life is an immediate impression of your contemplations. Be cautious, however. When you start to change how you figure, you will see that a portion of these terrible and prominent contemplations will attempt to meddle. Be solid. It has taken a long time for your brain to arrive in such a state and will require a significant period to transform it.

Proposals

1. Watch out for the prize.

2. Avoid individuals who will cut you down. (Condition)

3. Redundancy. Your mind needs steady sustenance.

4. Shut out any negative impact.

5. Steadiness. Take the necessary steps.

That rundown may appear to be little, however tailing it will guarantee that you get what you need. You need to comprehend that we, as individuals, are incredibly compelling. Pair this with our complex psychological examples; it is anything but difficult to perceive any reason why such a significant number of individuals don't have what they truly need.

If you stall out with this, make sure to consider youngsters. Watch kids. Watch how they follow what they need and multiple times out of 10 will have what they need, regardless of whether it is just a toy.

How to Instantly Hypnotize Someone to Get Anything You Want

The minute an individual happens to hear "Trance induction!", the individual in question is promptly immersed with the pictures of a detestable researcher, boasting in some rodent ridden basement, someplace somewhere down in the innards of the earth, where he is without left to control the brains and collections of men and control their wills to pursue his very own offering.

This prominent picture of trance induction had finished down the ages, as this craftsmanship was indicated utilized by learned people of old to put a wiped out man to rest before they treated him with careful blades.

As this kind of pertinent information was viewed as dark enchantment or some black magic by the uneducated basic man, the learned researchers, specialists, and clerics of that time encouraged the plan to guarantee that their mystery crafts of trance induction remained careful.

In any case, sleep induction is unquestionable, not dark artistry, nor is it gibberish. It happens to be an exceptionally all around idea out science, which uses the possibility of the trance specialist putting in an excellent recommendation in the subject's brain, in such a covert way, that he doesn't realize that he is being mesmerized. In such cases, the question starts to accept that the proposal is his thought.

The Power Of Conversational Hypnosis

This kind of trance induction goes under the Covert conversational spellbinding. An individual who is adept in the craft of conversational entrancing can figure out how to induce his potential customer, bank director, future boss, or some other subject before him to take a gander at things his way.

Covert conversational mesmerizing is a very much idea out methodology with which you figure out how to give your voice a chance to do all the "charming" and inducing. Your potential customer will envision that you are merely holding a customary discussion with him, yet you are gradually and relentlessly installing proposals into his intuitive, without his getting a notion of his having being mesmerized into seeing things his way.

This spellbinding must be finished by an individual who has figured out how to set up a definite affinity with his future customer.

Points of confinement Of Conversational Hypnosis

If the subject has a natural "personality obstruct" against the sales rep since he doesn't confide in him or like him, the psyche is undoubtedly not going to be open to any conversational trance induction. To every covert recommendation attempting to be embedded into the cerebrum, the subconscious is going to hurl a prompt reaction of a negative "Nyah." So all things considered, it will be inconceivable for you to mesmerize somebody without them understanding it.

In such cases, the individual you converse with is certainly not going to pursue your lead, nor is he going to be persuaded in purchasing only your items. Such an obstinate personality is additionally not going to state "yes" to nearly anything you let them know.

Along these lines, recall the first point — a fruitful backer of covert conversational entrancing figures out how to make himself preferred and trusted.

Performing Covert Hypnosis

The following significant purpose of covert conversational spellbinding is utilizing word designs in a cadenced manner to "install" a clandestine proposal into the brain of your subject. A relentless redundancy of such word designs at various interims is going to make the mind open to the thought you are nourishing it. Until obviously, your customer shakes hand upon the arrangement; after all, he was mesmerized into doing it!

Chapter six
How to Defend Yourself

Step by step instructions to Defend YourselfBelieve it or not, there are ways to give yourself the most obvious opportunity with regards to not turning into the following measures in the neighborhood wrongdoing figure index. Give yourself the edge, remaining sheltered as you venture out around taking care of your business or public activity. Pursue a couple of essential personal safety tips, and you increment your shot of remaining safe. Figure out how to shield yourself the savvy way, wherever conceivable.

Walk upstanding and glance around as you stroll along, be alert. If you look exchanged on and mindful, odds are you will be disregarded. They will search for a more straightforward objective.

Tune in for clamors close to you, e.g.:- individuals approaching you, and it most likely is an honest individual simply continuing ahead yet you know!

Attempt to abstain from tuning in to your iPod or Mp3 particularly around evening time, how might you know when you have hindered your hearing and consideration redirected somewhere else. Also the perils of vehicles and so on.

It is a great idea to have a cell phone with you, however, don't to have a long discussion about whether genuine or stage figured out how to attempt to show individuals you are associated. Again this occupies your consideration away from remaining mindful.

At the point when at all conceivable always tell family or companions where you are going and what time to expect you back, this isn't as specific individuals assume an attack of your security. Its fundamental safety common sense.

Always stay where individuals are near and in all around lit boulevards, Avoid going down back rear entryways or worthless modern domains, you get the image. Counteractive action is number one when figuring out how to shield yourself.

When you believe you are in risk of being pursued, go to the closest entryway. Thump hard and yell, clamor and consideration are the last things a future mugger or attacker needs.

Never go to the place of an individual you have recently met, meet in an unbiased spot where individuals are near, and you are remarkably unmistakable. Become more acquainted with them first and see the location they give you is their first home. Perhaps request a telephone number and check it in the book.

Most importantly, don't place yourself in potential threat. If you need to hang tight for a companion or relative to join you, at that point pause and be sheltered, it is vastly improved than winding up on a real existence bolster machine or more regrettable.

When somebody in a vehicle stops to ask headings, don't go up and put your head somewhere around the window. Remain back and glance around to check whether a conceivable second individual is near. This could be a diversion robbery endeavor, again whenever assaulted make as much commotion as you can.

At last, if you are defied, and requested your handbag, cell phone, or wallet. The best thing here is to toss the article they need to the side and behind them. This will give you essential seconds to perhaps flee and raise the alert.

You may much consider conveying a subsequent wallet or handbag, with an outdated Mastercard in it. Also, a little money to look genuine. All the above are reasonable and useful ways to remain safe, as you travel around doing your everyday business. This is the ideal way to figure out how to guard yourself, continuing caution, and staying away from a showdown.

How to Defend Yourself From an Attacker

FIRST - Fighting should just be utilized if all else fails. First attempt to prevail upon the assailant if that is conceivable. If they have a weapon and all they need is cash, its either conceivably your life or $50. Because you may realize how to disable an aggressor, does not imply that you might most likely damage everybody every time. You may have an off day, or you're drained, and after that, you mess up the opportunity to incapacitate the aggressor, and afterward, you get cut or perhaps killed. So at the end of the day, it is a lot more secure to give the assailant what they need, when they have a firearm that would be your best alternative.

SECOND - If the aggressor won't stop, then you should be prepared to safeguard yourself. First, you have to know about your environment consistently, so by this point, you should know where everything is around you. You have to get into a battling position with both of your hands up to square assaults. When you have your hands down, or in your line of vision, then you won't most likely square or divert the attacker's charges. Returning to continually monitoring your environment, it is a lot more secure to keep an article in the middle of you and your rival, for example, a refuse can and so on whatever might associate with you to prevent your aggressor from getting a straight line of assault on you.

THIRD - Know how to square and strike proficiently. I can not pressure that it is so imperative to figure out how to hit your assailant in essential spots, for example, the throat, ears, eyes, sunlight based plexus, crotches, or knees. If your assailant is coming directly at you, and you don't have the foggiest idea what to do complete a speedy yet fantastic kick to within the aggressor's knee. Regardless of how vast the aggressor is, if you strike his knee super hard, at that point his establishment will be disabled. No aggressor will be stressing over securing their knee, so you will quite often have that opportunity. Likewise, you NEED to realize how to BLOCK or at least DODGE. You would prefer not to be hit during an assault, and that is the place blocking or avoiding comes into spot. For instance, if they throw a jab, you can square and parallel advance to the outside of the punch. When you are outward of their punch, you are in the predominant position in light of the fact that your body is confronting them, yet they are not facing you which means in the event that they hit you that they won't most likely produce loads of intensity, However you will almost certainly since you are as yet confronting him and ready to strike the kidney's, ribs, or sanctuary. Parallel developments will be your best choice to evade an assault and put your body into an overwhelming position.

FOURTH - know to make an appropriate clench hand and how to get control into the majority of your strikes. When you throw a right hook, you should just hit with your forefinger's knuckle and your center finger's knuckle, this reduction the possibility of you harming your hand because your clench hand is currently aligned with your lower arm. Additionally, you have to get your entire body into an assault. When you throw a right hook with just your arm, it won't be that incredible, in any case when you get your hips and middle into the punch, at that point without a doubt your assailant will be harmed. If you toss a knee to the crotch or face, you should shoot your hips straight into the assault with your knee rather than merely raising your knee and hitting. This will guarantee that your aggressor does not have any desire to continue upsetting you since they will hurt!

FIFTH - ALWAYS remain insufficiently bright, all around populated regions. With more individuals around your odds of being assaulted are immensely decreased than if you were strolling along an obscure dark road with scarcely anybody or any traffic. What's more, when you have to stroll along a mysterious dark highway, at that point I urge we carry another person with you, and you need a solid ground-breaking walk and demonstrate that you look sure. If somebody looks sure and solid, they are more averse to be assaulted. Additionally, I advise purchasing pepper splash to keep in your sack or pocket consistently. Also, for your vehicle you ought to have something, for example, a bat just if you get hopped by more than one individual because there is scarcely anyone who could take on at least five folks exposed gave and win.

How to Defend Yourself in a Fight - Top Three Tips From a Self Defense Instructor

If you don't have the foggiest idea how to shield yourself in a battle, you would one be able today end up in genuine threat.

Not at all like what we see on TV or in the motion pictures, most genuine rough clashes:

1. Are Over In Less Than 10 Seconds;

2. Happen Rapidly and Unexpectedly;

3. Include Weapons as well as Surprisingly Vicious Tactics; and

4. End With One Party Seriously Injured

With no viable self-defense preparing, you could without much of a stretch end up on the losing end of a vicious battle - not somewhere that you ever need to be.

As a self-defense instructor and veteran of various savage clashes, I realize that a bit of preparing can go far. It could mean the contrast between leaving safe or leaving the scene in an emergency vehicle.

Given my preparation and experience, I offer the accompanying:

TOP THREE TIPS FOR DEFENDING YOURSELF IN A FIGHT

(1) STRIKE FIRST: If somebody shows, through their activities, that they have a goal to hurt you physically, don't sit tight for them to make that first move. When you foresee an immediate risk of peril, strike before it is past the point of no return.

2) TARGET THE VITAL AREAS: Strike at the most powerless focuses on the adversary's body. These are areas that can't be molded (toughened up, for example, the eyes, throat, sun oriented plexus, crotch, and knees. Assaulting any of these fundamental areas adequately will bring about quick torment as well as damage to your adversary, allowing you to catch up with different systems - or escape.

3) FOLLOW THROUGH AGGRESSIVELY: Unless you flee, DO NOT ease up after your underlying strike. The ideal approach to shield yourself is to be the assailant. Catch up with a blast of attacks. If you are able and sure with taking downs and holds, utilize them. Regardless, don't stop until you are 100% certain that the danger is killed.

A certified self-defense instructor can help you in building up the aptitudes and certainty that you have to guard yourself against any assailant and end a rough clash rapidly.

Try not to go one more day without realizing how to guard yourself in a battle.

Road Fighting Techniques - How to Defend Yourself Easily!

If you need to have the option to shield yourself, you can gain proficiency with the methods of urban self-defense to remain secure.

Regardless of the way that they're talented in the preparation they've experienced, many dark belts that run combative techniques, schools don't generally have any involvement in road battling and self-defense. Those of you who attempt to take classes at the YMCA or the exercise center trying to get some answers concerning road battling will only be hitting the sack in tedious developments.

Every one of these classes shows you how to do is perform moves that may seem surprising, yet when you genuinely need to battle somebody they will be futile; you should augment your preparation and strive to use these viable moves. You'll need to get the best possible hardware, such as competing gloves, a cup, better than average rec center shoes, a hand to hand fighting protective cap, and such to prepare for road battling. Legitimate, customary preparing consistently will give you the best probability that, if you get into a battle, you'll leave away as the victor.

You need to practice your brain just as your body. Getting amazed and found napping will be similarly as savage as not being physically arranged for a battle, so buckle down. Ensure you are knowledgeable about the genuine struggle so you can bargain and make do with the burdens battle includes. Keeping your quiet as opposed to being loaded up with dread will build your chances of winning. Come to the heart of the matter where you won't get diverted when hit in the appendages. When you have a touch of involvement added to your repertoire, begin not utilizing defensive rigging as you fight, enabling you to know your body notwithstanding a battle. Preparing your body to become acclimated with the impacts of a fight will help you more than anything on this occasion.

You genuinely need to exploit books, classes, and recordings that instruct legitimate road battling systems. If you would prefer not to transform into only one more dead body in the city, you must probably prepare your body adequately. With actual fighting, you'll genuinely be trying the breaking points of your substantial potential.

When you get assaulted, genuine competing will prepare you to have the option to anticipate each blow, be quiet in the circumstance, and enable you to endure a shot such that will keep you in the battle. You need to consistently prepare with the dynamic struggle to make your body and psyche. When you need to know how to road battle, you need to do fighting continuously.

Make sure to set objectives for yourself and train as hard and as frequently as possible. You can prepare yourself to gain proficiency with the impulses of battle as you wear your defensive hardware. Locate a perfect, calm spot to make your battling aptitudes in harmony. If you keep it correct when you figure out how to battle, you'll be better prepared to deal with yourself in a genuine battle circumstance.

How to Defend Yourself From Getting Raped

Assault. This single word speaks to one of the terrifying encounters a lady will ever confront. In spite of the awfulness, the word summons it is significant for a lady to realize that there are steps they can take to enable themselves to forestall a sexual assault. The motivation behind this part is to give lady approaches to avoid rape, and give women devices to protect themselves should they ever be assaulted by an aggressor.

Like some other wrongdoing assault is frequently wrongdoing of chance. It is in this manner significant that a lady knows about her surroundings consistently. When strolling in parking areas or carports, walk unquestionably and at an energetic pace. Be cautious when individuals stop to approach headings or to request cash. Continuously answer from separation and never get excessively near somebody who is addressing you from a vehicle. Be additional mindful you are in a domain where liquor is being served. When you are in a club or bar, never leave your beverage unattended. If for reasons unknown you do go, request a new drink when you return. Never acknowledge a drink from somebody you don't have the foggiest idea. Above all, trust your impulses. Numerous women allow themselves to be set in perilous circumstance because of a paranoid fear of being discourteous or seeming suspicious. If time gives you a pure inclination, there is most likely a reason. Tune in to that feeling and act appropriately.

In spite of your earnest attempts at evading peril, you may wind up in a circumstance where you are eye to eye with an attacker and assault appears to be up and coming. In cases like this, it is imperative to stay calm and confident. Attackers assault because they ache for power and looking to fulfill that requirement for power by mortifying and controlling another person. Crying and asking will give the result he is searching for, and these practices will probably urge him to do the assault. Try to attract thoughtfulness regarding yourself by hollering fire. Fire is a superior decision than "Help" or "Assault" since encompassing individuals may waver to engage with legitimate issues or a conceivable hazardous circumstance. Shouting "fire" will draw the consideration of spectators making the consideration be attracted to you and the attacker. A particular caution can be viable in both attracting thoughtfulness regarding yourself just as making physical torment the attacker's ears. If nobody is around trying serenely talking, slowing down for a time, or tell the aggressor, you have an STD.

At the point when physically shielding yourself against a male culprit, the main safeguard move that strikes a chord is to either kick or knee the man in the crotch. This isn't a fitting resistance move. It is simple for a man to see this move coming, and he is generally on a gatekeeper for it. It is barely noticeable this territory, and a bombed endeavor will annoy the man further. Stepping hard on the highest point of the foot or kicking the shins or the knee top is similarly as powerful and a lot simpler to execute effectively. Spots like the YMCA and neighborhood law enforcement organizations can regularly give data on self-preservation classes that can enable you to learn other physical self-protection moves.

There are numerous gadgets available that give no deadly types of self-protection. Pepper sprays can weaken a criminal without causing changeless physical harm. They are lightweight simple to utilize and can be used from a good ways from the culprit when picking a protection shower search for one that contains an OC detailing. Not at all like different sorts of pepper sprays, items with OC formulations cause physical responses inside the body and will be successful on all individuals including the individuals who are drunk or in a perspective that makes them careless in regards to physical agony.

Stun firearms are another non deadly yet exceedingly powerful self-preservation choice. Like OC pepper sprays, stun weapons accomplish something beyond cause physical torment. They cause disturbances in the skeletal, sensory system that will cripple a potential attacker for as long as 45 minutes. One inconvenience of stun weapons is that they do necessitate that an individual makes physically contacts the assailant with the stun firearm. It is along these lines imperative to consider the size and length of the stun weapon. It is a smart thought to physically stun the aggressor first by utilizing the resistance move referenced before in this article, for example, kicking the shins or stepping the foot.

When you are in a circumstance when you are in peril of an assault, you reserve the privilege to utilize anything available to you to ensure yourself. The conceivable weapon can be your vehicle keys a handle of a brush or items in your shopping sack. Regurgitating on you assailant could likewise repulse him. While you reserve the privilege to shield yourself, be careful in utilizing whatever can be viewed as a hostile weapon, for example, a firearm or blade. State laws shift broadly on the agreeableness of the utilization of these weapons. Regardless of whether no charges get squeezed against you for utilizing these weapons in self-preservation, you may wind up being sued by your assailant for harming him while he was trying to assault you!

The world can be a terrifying and hazardous spot. Learning how to deal with these circumstances can empower us to remain safe despite the threat.

How to Defend Yourself - In All Matters

Ladies are as yet attempting to locate their exact spot that relates to the worth they add to the general public. As moms, they sustain the youthful. As spouses, they adjust. As sisters, they counsel. As girls, they watch out for their older folks.

A noteworthy reason for stress for a lady nowadays is assaulted by others. They have to protect themselves against these assaults. Presently attacks need not be just physical. First ladies ought to comprehend the kinds of attacks they face both at home, in the public arena, and at work. Here are the most basic ones and a few hints on the most proficient method to protect yourself.

1. PHYSICAL - These can be by a mugger, an abuser, a violater or (in all honesty) from over-brutal kids. It can emerge from complete outsiders to individuals who are near you.

Tips: learn self-protection. Maintain a strategic distance from spots you can be defenseless -, for example, obscured parking garages or stairs, late-night lifts and unusual pieces of a town. Likewise, learn "gaze intently at" strategy. Assault from a grown-up ought to be countered first by not demonstrating any dread because an assailant is extremely a weakling and a harasser on a fundamental level. The minute you show you are not apprehensive and are fit for protecting yourself, you have won a large portion of the fight. Utilize realistically. When the individual is intoxicated and waving a firearm, walk or flee, or call for assistance. Assault by kids ought to never be endured even though guardians may downplay it. Kids who discover excitement in hitting or scratching will turn progressively rough. So once more, gaze intently at and immovably state no. Next time the tyke attempts to kick, immovably get hold of his arm and land NO! Regardless of whether it is another person's youngster. It is never a smart thought to whine to the parent first - manage it yourself, at that point, gripe. That way, the tyke will discover that you are not to be played with.

2. MENTAL - this may happen in the workplace when your manager or associate is attempting to be a twitch or practice mental torment on you. It can likewise be from your mate or relatives.

Tips: don't give the tormentor a chance to push your catches. The most noticeably awful thing you can do is lose self-assurance due to what is said- - that is absolutely what the tormentors need from you, and afterward, they have you where they need you. Solidly, serenely express your position. If the other party participates in yelling or shouting, let them completion and after that state, "I figure you should quiet down and carry on like a grown-up proficient I realize you can be. Give us a chance to visit when you are thinking and talking reasonably, will we?" After two seconds, leave. Likewise, search for an example of badgering and don't be hesitant to propose advising, or on account of the office, go to Human Resources or the following level director. Under the law, a chief can't disregard objections and needs to make a move.

3. Monetary - this can be through tricks or relatives or companions "mooching."

Tips: never work together exclusively on trust. This incorporates contributing cash (recall what occurred the kindred who duped companions who helped with him and brought them down for billions? These companions indiscriminately confided in him and never addressed things that were not typical in speculation the executives. So get your work done. It merits the additional cash to pay a bookkeeper, a legal counselor, or even a legal bookkeeper to look at the plan for authenticity and foundation.

The most effective method to Defend Yourself With a Stun Gun

If you are ever stood up to by an aggressor while strolling, running, or getting in or out of your vehicle, you can effectively protect yourself with a stun weapon. A stun firearm is a little electrical gadget with two short terminals reaching out from its surface. It is small enough to fit into the palm of your hand. Whenever activated, it produces a high voltage; however, practically no amperage. This is the reason it is non-deadly and unfit to shock anybody. The amperage is the thing that causes severe damage, not the voltage.

A stun weapon will in a split second immobilize an attacker with a three to five-second touch. The high voltage immediately converts blood sugar into lactic corrosive. This right away drains the attacker's muscle vitality, and the assailant is left without the capacity to move. Simultaneously, the neurological driving forces which coordinate and controls muscle development is intruded. The attacker further loses balance, moves toward becoming befuddle and can never again stand. This condition will last from five to ten minutes. You ought to have all that could be needed time to get to a protected area.

Stun weapons are increasingly viable when an attacker is contacted over the waste line to the upper shoulders. The whole body will be influenced. If only an arm or leg is reached, you risk merely affecting that piece of the body. At different occasions, a potential assault might be hindered by merely releasing the stun weapon in mid-air. The cathodes produce a loud scaring popping sound.

It doesn't make a difference how huge an assailant is or whether the attacker is affected by liquor or opiates; it will be successful. It makes an emotional, chemical response and meddles with the aggressor's neurological framework. This is something outside the ability to control an aggressor. Will and quality are superfluous. A model would put an elephant under sedation. Regardless of how enormous or powerful an elephant is, a little sedative spot can cut it down.

It is likewise viable and will effectively go through garments. For whatever length of time that the battery is charged, it very well may be terminated on various occasions at numerous attackers. If external contact you, there will be no electric stun or chargeback to you. The amperage is too low to even think about creating a voyaging circuit. The voltage remains between the terminals and to the assailant. The higher the voltage rating of a stun weapon, the quicker it will debilitate the objective.

CONCLUSION

If you have concluded that you need to have the option to safeguard yourself and your friends and family, you have settled on an excellent choice. In this day and age, where wrongdoing rates are continually rising, it is imperative to have the option to shield yourself and rapidly escape a possibly unsafe circumstance. Self-protection isn't tied in with turning into a hooligan that uses every opportunity possible to stir something up so he can test his most current systems and check whether they work, although individuals like this exist it is unquestionably not the attitude of the ordinary military craftsman.

Self-preservation is tied in with counteracting dangerous circumstances before occurring. You can do this by taking preventive estimates like maintaining a strategic distance from specific areas and neighborhoods. Abstain from staring at individuals who resemble offenders and seem as though they are searching for the inconvenience. The following stage is the point at which an encounter does occur, and it is still at the verbal level you can protect yourself by rapidly finishing the discourse verbally and leaving.

The way to verbal self-preservation isn't demonstrating that you are frightened and not inciting the aggressor. You can generally apologize to assuage the vicious individual's personality and let him feel prevalent. Anyway, a few people don't get insight and can all of a sudden assault you even though you pursue all the above advances.

This is the place the last degree of self-preservation becomes an integral factor, physically shielding yourself. This should occur after you have attempted the various measures despite everything you feel that you can get assaulted any minute or if the aggressor has just begun the physical encounter. There ought to be two things in your mind when the confrontation turns physical. The first is to end the battle as fast as could be allowed, and the second is to escape the hazardous circumstance.

It doesn't make a difference what military craftsmanship class you take as long as it centers around consummation the battle rapidly by all methods possible and after that is leaving. You ought to never feel remorseful about hitting an aggressor as he will hurt you gravely inside seconds if you delay. You generally need to offer him the chance to stop his activities and let you go, clearly as long as the physical showdown hasn't occurred.

Thanks for giving me confidence and took my book, if you want to read other fantastic books visit my library ...

You won't regret it!

Made in the USA
Middletown, DE
03 March 2020